UNITED
WE BRAND

UNITED
WE BRAND

How to Create a Cohesive Brand That's Seen,
Heard, and Remembered

MIKE MOSER

HARVARD BUSINESS SCHOOL PRESS
BOSTON, MASSACHUSETTS

978-1-57851-798-5 (ISBN 13)

Library of Congress Cataloging-in-Publication Data

Moser, Mike, 1953–
    United we brand : how to create a cohesive brand that's seen, heard,
and remembered / Mike Moser.
        p. cm.
    Includes bibliographical references and index.
    ISBN 1-57851-798-2 (alk. paper)
    1. Brand name products. 2. New products—Management. I. Title.
HD69.B7 M67 2003
658.8'27—dc21

                                                        2002152610

The paper used in this publication meets the requirements of the
American National Standard for Permanence of Paper for Publications
and Documents in Libraries and Archives Z39.48-1992.

CONTENTS

PREFACE

This book is a direct result of more than twenty years of experience in advertising, design, and brand communication. My first years in advertising were spent at two agencies: the first two years at Altschiller, Reitzfeld and Jackson in New York (voted the hottest U.S. agency under $25 million in 1980) and nine years at Chiat/Day Advertising (voted the agency of the decade in the 1980s). I was intimately involved with some major marketing wars of that decade: Apple against IBM, California Cooler against Seagram's and Gallo, Worlds of Wonder against Hasbro and Mattel, Reebok against Nike, and Dell against IBM and Compaq. In each case, I was working on the brand that had less money, less awareness, and less of a brand than its competitors. Because of that experience, I grew to understand the competitive advantage of having a core set of corporate values, a microscopically focused brand message, a distinct brand personality, and a consistent set of brand icons. Those experiences were invaluable in the writing of this book.

The next phase of my experience came in 1990. Jay Chiat enabled my partners (Fred Goldberg and Brian O'Neill) and me to buy out the San Francisco office of Chiat/Day, and the agency Goldberg Moser O'Neill (GMO) was born. The responsibility of having to communicate the essence of our clients' brands while creating a successful brand for ourselves refined my branding experience even further. As an agency, Goldberg Moser O'Neill grew from 70 people and $70 million in billing to 300 people and $450 million in billing in nine short (or is that long?) years. As co-creative directors, Brian O'Neill and I split the accounts. During that time, I was overseeing the Dell Computer and Kia Motors America accounts, in addition to several other, smaller accounts. Given the rate of our growth, the growth of our clients (Dell and Cisco were two of the world's fastest-growing companies in the 1990s), and the constantly changing personnel at both the agency and the firms of our clients, it became critical to have some sort of brand document in place to ensure brand consistency. I then decided to create a booklet that would give everyone working on each account a sense of direction and a gut feeling for the brand. I wanted the document to be simple, clear, and usable so that I wouldn't need to have the same branding conversation with each individual working on the account. When I couldn't find an existing template in the marketplace, I created my own. The booklet, which I called a brand roadmap, was designed to be a down-to-earth, practical guide to help both clients and agency people make day-to-day branding decisions.

When the first brand roadmap I designed, for Kia Motors, was well received, I started creating them for more and more clients. Among these clients were Cisco Systems, Dell, start-up companies like CarClub.com and ShareWave, regional retail establishments like Stuart Anderson's Black Angus restaurants, local establishments like Jerome's Bar-B-Que, and image-driven companies like Beringer Winery and David Grisman's Acoustic Disc Records.

After leaving Goldberg Moser O'Neill and the advertising business in 1999, I started donating my time and talents to schools, nonprofit organizations, and small businesses that were having a hard time being seen and heard in this marketing-saturated culture. I used the same brand roadmap template for them that I had used for the larger clients. The template helped these organizations focus their attention and redirect some of their marketing dollars to the messages that mattered. It particularly helped schools and nonprofits produce marketing materials that accurately reflected their brand and not just the creative whim of whatever volunteer was doing the brochure, invitation, or newsletter. The brand roadmap proved itself over and over again.

IS THIS BRAND ROADMAP A WHOLE NEW IDEA?

Since doing these brand roadmaps and writing this book, I've discovered that the brand roadmap isn't necessarily a new idea. Many large corporations, branding experts, brand consultancies, and multinational corporate identity and advertising firms already use names and techniques similar to the brand roadmap. In various forms, it's known by names like brand print, brand optimization, brand DNA, brand intent, brand visioning, and other iterations too varied and numerous to list here. But unfortunately for you, the templates tend to be proprietary ones used by organizations to create cohesive brand strategies for their own clients in the marketplace. Consequently, thousands of companies and organizations have no access to the templates. These groups lack the money, time, or knowledge that would allow access to the proprietary templates or to the talent that could develop such templates. The step-by-step process in this book will help you achieve some of the same brand insights, brand focus, and brand consistency delivered by many of those proprietary formulas.

WHO CAN BENEFIT FROM THIS BOOK?

If you can find yourself in this list, this book is for you.

The lots-of-hats people. People who have many roles in their organization—owners of small to medium-sized businesses, directors of nonprofits, and freelance consultants—find that the brand roadmap helps them focus on the critical branding elements in their business. It gives them insights into the brand attributes that will help differentiate them in the marketplace. The brand roadmap also helps them focus their marketing on the ideas that matter and gives them an off-the-shelf template for a distinctive, cohesive brand identity in the marketplace.

Brand novices, business experts. Many brand "novices" have a degree in business and are extremely competent at the strategic aspects of branding—brand values and brand message. These same people, however, feel woefully inadequate when it comes to the executional aspects of branding, like the brand personality and brand icons. This book gives these business-people a language and way to understand and articulate those aspects of their brand. In many cases these people are from organizations that can't afford the best and the brightest in the world of advertising, design, and brand consultancy, but they long for that level of branding expertise for their company. This book gives them the tools to capture that expertise and create a brand roadmap. With the brand roadmap in hand, these managers can delegate the day-to-day branding decisions to someone else in their organization so that they can get back to the business of their business.

Brand experts who need to communicate to brand novices.
Research has shown that brand mission, vision, and values
are generally understood among senior managers, but that
the same understanding doesn't permeate the rest of the
organization.[1] For managers who understand branding—
usually CEOs and marketing directors for national and
multinational corporations—the brand roadmap becomes a
great tool for explaining their brand to the people within
their organization. There are few if any existing templates to
help senior managers communicate the essence of their
brand internally. The brand roadmap accomplishes this job.
It also presents branding information in a way that's easy to
read, easy to implement, and eminently practical for the people within the organization, from the receptionist (sometimes
people's first contact with a brand) to the board of directors.

Brand novices, business novices. For people who are truly new to
the business world and all aspects of branding, the brand
roadmap helps them quickly arrive at an understanding of
brand focus, brand cohesiveness, and effective brand communication. Sometimes these novices are people who leave larger
businesses to start their own business. Many times they're
students who are majoring in marketing, advertising, business, or design and can benefit immensely from this "Cliffs
Notes" version of achieving brand unity and simple, clear
brand communication.

THIS IS NOT A COMPLETE BOOK ON BRANDING

Despite this book's strengths in helping companies focus and create
meaningful and powerful brand communications, it's far from being

a complete book on branding. In fact, what it doesn't cover could fill a book—a book like David Aaker's *Building Strong Brands.*[2] *United We Brand* doesn't cover such topics as brand architecture, co-branding, brand extension, multi-branding, global branding, segmented marketing, or brand equity management. Nor is this book meant to be a substitute for the detailed, scholarly research and business case studies that span a whole range of specific branding issues. It certainly isn't a substitute for getting practical experience in brand management at a major corporation like Procter & Gamble, for example. As you're reading this book, be forewarned that it's going to be light on scholarly research and heavy on information that's passed through personal experience and marketplace feedback.[3] With that in mind, if you run across ideas in this book that are reminiscent of magazine articles you've encountered, books you've read, or even articles you may have written, I may have inadvertently picked up some of those ideas through the prism of other people's knowledge or experience. I've worked with some amazing branding people over the last twenty years; I may have forgotten where I initially heard the idea. In that case, I apologize. Throughout my career, my modus operandi has been to latch on to whatever ideas would work for my clients, without my necessarily worrying about who came up with the idea or documenting where the idea came from. Constant deadlines and nonstop problem solving over the years have, unfortunately, blurred my memory. Whenever I do remember or recognize a direct contribution from a colleague, a speaker, an author, a book, or an article, I certainly give credit where credit is due. Not documenting my sources might also come from my "scholarly" background, which consists of graduating from Los Angeles Trade-Technical College with an associate's degree in commercial art. I never went to a four-year school, never had to write a thesis, and never took a course in business or marketing. The driving force in my career has been practicality, which you'll find is pretty much my default position on everything having to do with brand communication. So you can rest assured that whatever you read in this book has worked for a number of successful companies in the marketplace.

A FEW WORDS ON A WORD USED THROUGHOUT THE BOOK

Throughout this book, I use the word *company*. I struggled with whether I should use this word, because of my own experience with schools, nonprofits, and small businesses. The word *company* is not how these organizations tend to describe themselves. But I felt it was better to use one word that was consistent and succinct rather than trying to be all things to all people. So a line that reads "Branding is a valuable tool for every company" should be interpreted as "Branding is a valuable tool for every company, school, nonprofit, service, small (or medium-sized or large) business, corporation, megaconglomacom.com, or other organization." I'll let you substitute your own word for *company*.

I DIDN'T DO THIS ALONE

There are so many people to thank for their insights, experience, and mentoring throughout my career. I couldn't have achieved what I've achieved in the communications business without their abilities to communicate their knowledge and experience to me.

Cheri Ramey first taught me how to introduce ideas and concepts into every design, from address labels to packaging to album covers. Her unending energy and enthusiasm were contagious and taught me to come up with new ideas until I ran out of time.

Bob Reitzfeld, David Altschiller, and Dick Jackson gave me my first job in advertising and allowed me to be a human sponge for that New York style of advertising: direct, smart, honest, and effective. I couldn't have gotten a better start to my career, and the portfolio I took with me after two years enabled me to get a job at another hot agency back in California: Chiat/Day Advertising.

The late Jay Chiat created an advertising/marketing environment where the best and brightest could become better and brighter. The long list of my influences at Chiat/Day reads like a who's who of advertising: Lee Clow, Hy Yablonka, Steve Hayden, Gary Johns, Jeff Gorman, Brent Thomas, Rick Boyko, Yvonne Smith, Bill Hamilton, M. T. Rainey, Jane Newman, and a constantly revolving cast of talent who inevitably ended up starting their own ad agencies, design firms, film production companies, and branding consultancies. I'd particularly like to single out Lee Clow, a creative director's creative director, who taught me how to execute the heck out of an idea and really create a visual distinctiveness in the marketplace. Thanks to Lee's direction, I was twice voted San Francisco Art Director of the Year. He was also the first person to encourage me to write. He had read a memo I had written to the agency, and he liked it and told me so. Because of his comment, I ended up writing over forty thought pieces over the next few years (they ended up in our new business/new employee booklet, called the Moser Memos). Each memo was on a specific topic, ranging from brand personality to selling creative work to creating simple, black-and-white branding differentiation.

I'd like to thank Fred Goldberg, my partner at Goldberg Moser O'Neill, who had a passion for excellence, an incredible mind for business, and an unerring intuition for powerful marketing strategies. I learned a lot of what I learned about business and branding from his insights.

Brian O'Neill, as my writer partner for seven years and business partner for nine more years, was always my better half. His ability to write well, see the big picture, and connect emotionally with his readers, employees, clients, and friends was an unending lesson in how to remain both talented and "nice" in a highly stressful business. During the 1980s, we won more than 250 national and international advertising awards together. We couldn't have accomplished that feat without his great talents. I also wouldn't have taken a chance and started an ad agency if he had not been aboard. The chemistry we had together was rare. To this day, I'm sure that more than half the stuff in this book is a mirror of his influences and insights.

My other GMO former partners, Catrina McAuliffe (brand planner), Mike Massaro (account manager and COO), and Camille Johnson (media maven), provided insights, experience, comments, and feedback that made me a much more complete marketing person. We worked on some of the highest-profile, fastest-growing accounts in the world and came through the process a bit shell-shocked, but better friends and much better branding people. I couldn't have written this book without rubbing shoulders (literally, in the case of our many trips down to Dell) with their talent.

Special thanks to Dave Woodside, who was always a great sounding board for my ideas and constantly made the writing style in my memos simpler and clearer.

My friend and business author, Louis Patler, helped me put together the original proposal for this book and introduced me to his agent, John Willig.

John Willig helped me redo my book proposal and got me a contract with Harvard Business School Press.

Harvard Business School Press took a chance on a neophyte writer and had the good sense to team me up with a senior editor—Suzanne Rotondo—who always brought out the best in my ideas.

The incredible difference between the first and last drafts of this book is due in large part to her honesty, encouragement, and ability to hone in on the important aspects of this very broad topic called branding. Jacqueline Murphy stepped into the process during the peer review and editorial board phase and really focused my thoughts in the right direction. It's a much clearer book because of her clarity. Editorial coordinator Astrid Sandoval made all the communication with HBSP as efficient, informative, and pleasurable as possible. She also organized the whole peer review process, which helped me make this book a much more focused, targeted, and useful book for people. Copy editor Patty Boyd made sure that my voice remained intact throughout the final copy editing process, and made me appear a much better writer than I am. Manuscript editor Karen Medlin made sure all the disparate pieces—design, copy, artwork, and captions—came together seamlessly. Design director Mike Fender gave me the opportunity to design the cover of this book. I gave him a hand and we came out with my thumbprint. I thank Hollis Heimbouch and every other person at HBSP whom I've dealt with during the writing of this book. They've all been extremely smart and helpful. I can see why they have the brand they do. I feel very fortunate to be associated with all of them. The six anonymous peer reviewers really helped me put my book into context with other branding books and spent the time and effort to clearly articulate their thoughts and impressions. This book became a much better book because of their input.

Thanks to all the clients I've worked with over the years and who have let me learn the business of branding on their dollar and with their brands. They were my real-world professors. My gratitude goes to the hundreds of talented copywriters, art directors, producers, directors, editors, musicians, planners, researchers, and media and account people I've interacted with and learned from over the years.

My ex-wife, Frances Whitnall, endured eighteen years of my sleepless nights, constant air travel, and 24/7 problem solving. Having been an art director herself and a terrific conceptual thinker, she understood the business of advertising and made my work better than it would have been without her input and ideas. She was also a great stay-at-home mom, keeping the family together and giving me the stability I needed to learn what I learned, and experience what I experienced, to be able to write this book.

My kids—Mallory, Jack, and Henry—teach me every day the value of creativity and fresh insights and the importance of humor in everything we do.

My dad, a top salesman, taught me how to sell effectively. Because of him, I've always considered myself a salesperson. I respect the discipline and knowledge it takes to do it well. He also showed me the value of relevant and powerful product demonstrations, by creating them himself out in the garage after hours. He always thought big. I'm fortunate to have inherited a bit of his philosophy and point of view.

My mom's Irish common sense and practical problem solving were always in the back of my mind, keeping my ideas and solutions grounded in reality. It turned out to be a valuable asset in the world of marketing communications, where companies tend to put way too much emphasis on "image" and "impression management" and not enough on pragmatism and consistent character.

I would like to thank you all. I couldn't have written this book without you.

UNITED
WE BRAND

ONE

You're Five Steps Away from Having a Customized Brand

If there is any discrepancy between the reality of your company and its perception in the marketplace, you need a brand roadmap. If there are people inside and outside of your organization who don't understand the passion and values of your organization, you need a brand roadmap. If you have a strong brand and need to communicate it simply and clearly to new employees, board members, or suppliers, you need a brand roadmap. If your marketing materials don't accurately reflect the mission or values of your organization, you need a brand roadmap. It doesn't matter whether you're a business owner, a director of a nonprofit organization, a small-business manager, a new entrepreneur, a middle or a senior manager—you need a brand roadmap. A *brand roadmap* is a document that is unique to each company and that serves as a template for you and everyone else to follow to ensure brand consistency. In essence, the roadmap will give everyone a clear vision of the company's brand.

As a newcomer to the U.S. automobile industry in the early 1990s, Kia Motors America benefited from such a roadmap approach. At the time, I was creative director on the account, and as a result of having a booklet that captured the essence of their brand, Kia was able to consistently articulate to all its various suppliers, dealers, customers, public relations people, marketing people, and Korean management the principles that would enable the company to succeed in the marketplace for years to come. This brand consistency enabled the automaker to grow from a mere twenty dealerships in the United States in 1993 to over six hundred by 2000.

During their incredible growth spurts in the 1990s, Dell Computer and Cisco Systems also benefited from the roadmap approach. This approach has worked for companies as diverse as Fortune 100 companies, local restaurants, local nonprofits, national retail chains, start-up companies, and schools that have been around for eighty years. What the brand roadmap will accomplish for you will be the creation of a unique, consistent, and trustworthy brand that is not dependent on the whims of any single individual, but on the internal and external identities of your company.

WHY IT'S CALLED A BRAND ROADMAP

I use the term *brand roadmap* because the first time I used this approach to customize a brand was for a car company, Kia Motors America. A roadmap seemed like the thematically right thing to do. The "roadmap" for Stuart Anderson's Black Angus restaurants was called a brand trail map. The "roadmap" for the Corporation for

Supportive Housing was called a brand blueprint. The name doesn't matter nearly as much as the process and the thinking.

I like the term *roadmap*, however, because people intuitively understand the concept of what a roadmap does and when to use it. A roadmap gives them a visual snapshot of the world they want to travel in. It can be picked up any time to clarify a misstep. It allows a person to get from point A to point B any number of ways. The analogy of a roadmap seems to give a company permission to find its own route, its own distinctive path, to brand nirvana. For the purpose of this book, let's call it a brand roadmap. You can call it whatever you like when you finalize your document in the last chapter.

Now that we've looked at what a brand roadmap is, let's examine why it's becoming an essential tool for companies nowadays.

WHY YOU NEED A BRAND ROADMAP

Think of the brand roadmap as a common cure for brand schizophrenia, a term I picked up from my former partner Fred Goldberg. A split can occur because every company has both an internal and an external identity. The internal part of the company has to do with the company itself: how well it knows itself, what its values are, how consistently it acts in accordance with those values, and what it really believes about the quality of its products and services. This internal sense of itself and the value system that goes with it is the area we'll explore in chapter 2, Core Brand Values.

The external part of a company's identity is how well it connects and relates to others. The better it knows itself and what it stands for, the better it connects with everyone who comes in contact with the brand: investors, customers, suppliers, employees, prospects, even competitors. We'll explore the external expressions of the company's identity in chapters 3 (Core Brand Message), 4 (Brand Personality), and 5 (Brand Icons).

When the internal and external identities are the same, the brand is strong. When the internal and external identities are inconsistent, or at odds, the brand is weak. You see examples of inconsistent identities all the time with companies that say they value customer service, but then make you wait forty-five minutes on their tech-support line. A company's products, services, and marketing materials are the tangible criteria people use to determine how "whole" the brand is, versus how fragmented or schizophrenic it might be. When a brand is considered whole—it knows itself, acts consistently on a core set of values, and communicates consistently and truthfully both internally and externally—then that brand is considered trustworthy and reliable. It has what is termed brand integrity.

A split between a company's internal and external identities is likely to occur if the company's values and mission statements are created by one group of people and the brand message, brand personality, and brand icons are created by another group. In the gap that results, something is usually missing: the essence of the brand. This book aims to help you avoid this gap. Unifying the process of creating values, message, personality, and icons will help you create a consistent, cohesive identity both inside and outside your company. As Nicholas Ind states in his book *Living the Brand,* "Brands come to life when the boundaries between internal and external blur."[1] Going through the brand roadmap exercises will help you create the consistency that will bring your brand to life.

TIMES CHANGE, BRANDING CHANGES

You may be wondering why having a consistent brand inside and outside the company is important when you can just tell people what you want to tell them and let it go at that. In the past, such an approach worked for companies. As recently as the 1980s, companies could craft a singular message and create the impression they wanted in the marketplace because there were fewer companies, fewer media outlets, and less skepticism in the marketplace. They were like the Wizard of Oz, bellowing out edicts over a few channels of network television and radio. This approach doesn't work as well today. Information flows too freely, and there are too many contact points in the marketplace for a company to hide what's really going on behind the scenes. Thanks to the Internet and a news-starved media, everyone has a permanent backstage pass to see what's really going on. People can know as much about you as you know about them. It's becoming a two-way street to truthfulness. For example, Nike advertises that it empowers kids, women, old people, and minorities. Meanwhile, more and more people have learned that some of its Southeast Asian manufacturers disempower—guess who?—kids, women, old people, and minorities.[2] If this discrepancy isn't addressed, then the brand suffers. The relationship between Nike and everyone who comes in contact with the brand is on shaky ground because the core values are on shaky ground. Honesty has crept into the relationship, and the honesty needs to be dealt with. So in a world where information is power and disclosure is fast becoming the norm, it's critical that your brand be as honest and truthful as possible. Being honest and truthful while you're working your way through this brand roadmap process is a great way to start the process of creating a brand with integrity.

YOU KNOW MORE ABOUT BRANDING THAN YOU THINK

Most people in business know most of what they need to know to do effective branding and create a valued brand. They know that branding is important, but the sheer volume of information available on the subject overwhelms them. The problem isn't a lack of information; it's finding a way to funnel all that information into a usable form. That's what this book, and the brand roadmap in particular, is designed to do. It will enable you to take all those nuggets of knowledge you already know and put them into a form that you, and anyone else who needs to communicate your brand, can utilize on a daily basis. You will end up with a workable, easy-to-understand, and easy-to-use brand roadmap.

THE ORDER OF THIS BOOK MATTERS

Step by step, this book will take you through the process of creating a unique brand in the marketplace. Each of the five steps, described in chapters 2 through 6, will build on the step before it, enabling you to create a brand roadmap that's customized for your company.

Chapter 2 will help you articulate your company's core brand values. Once you decide on three or four core values, everything that follows in the brand roadmap will be based on those values. Those values will be the foundation of every decision your company makes—from the kind of people you hire, to the kinds of customers you pursue, to the partners you choose, to the marketing decisions you make—and they'll be the pillars of any message you deliver. Since core brand values are the foundation your brand is built upon, we'll go through some exercises to make sure that the foundation is solid.

Chapter 3 will help you create and fine-tune your core brand message, the key message that captures your company's reason for being. Once that core message is put down in writing—preferably in blood (I'm kidding, but just barely)—all other messages will support and add credibility to that message.

Chapter 4 will help you determine your brand personality. This personality will determine what tone and attitude your organization is going to use to deliver your core brand message. The chapter will also help you create a personality that acts and sounds like a real person instead of one of those idealistic pseudo-personalities generally pieced together by an ad hoc committee over some weekend corporate retreat.

Chapter 5 will help clarify and prioritize your brand icons. You'll find that the process you went through to understand your brand values, message, and brand personality will help you evaluate and choose appropriate colors, typefaces, voice-overs, logos, layouts, music, signage, and architecture for your brand. You'll develop some objective criteria to evaluate areas that tend to be very subjective. Having been both a passionate, young art director and a creative director of passionate, young art directors and designers, I know how emotionally charged and irrational a discussion about colors, design, and visual techniques can get. Not only does the forest get lost for the trees, but the trees get lost for the branches, and the branches get lost for the bark. A brand roadmap will give you a focus and a vocabulary that can help bring some sanity to those emotionally charged situations.

Chapter 6 will take you through the process of putting together your own brand roadmap. The exercises and format will make sure that all the separate pieces—core values, brand message, brand personality, and brand icons—are working together. This chapter will help you eliminate redundancies, smooth out any inconsistencies, and make the document as lean and as pragmatic as possible.

It may not seem apparent at first, but the order of this book matters. Too many companies start at the wrong end of the process. They start with the design of their logo or a brand icon and work their way back to their core message. Or they say, "I want something funny," and suddenly, their brand personality becomes their company. A lot of the dot-coms fell into this trap, or dot-comedies as author Louis Patler likes to call them. You'd laugh along with one of their commercials, but would ask yourself, "Who are they? What do they do? Why should I care?" The next thing you know, they're gone. Ha-ha.

So please take the time to follow the process in the order it's laid out in this book. The order is designed to help others who come in contact with your brand understand how they can apply their specific talents to your overall brand plan. If you don't follow a prescribed sequence, you run the risk of having your brand roadmap feel as pieced together as that first collage you made in the third grade. You'll love it, your mom will love it, but it will come across as what it is—a pieced-together roadmap that only a mother could love.

AVOIDING BRAND MYOPIA

Before we delve into the details of creating a brand roadmap, let's consider a common affliction called brand myopia.[3] Brand myopia is the practice of shutting out all the possibilities for your brand because of a preconceived notion that the only lessons applicable to your category are those learned from other companies in your category. You see it all the time: Car companies study other car companies, computer companies study other computer companies, ice cream companies study other ice cream companies, and restaurants copy other restaurants.

Because of this myopia, car companies all end up making essentially the same car, with the same service contracts and the same warranties. Computer companies all talk about what's on the chip and on the cheap. Ice cream companies end up with, pardon the wordplay, vanilla marketing, and every restaurant—even McDonald's—has some form of Caesar salad.

So when you're going through this book, try to step outside your category every now and then. If you're a computer company, imagine you're a car company and see what you'd do. Or study a particular car company and see what's been done. If you're a local retailer like a bookstore, restaurant, or hardware store, pretend you're a national image-oriented brand—perfume, wine, fashion—and see how you'd solve your problem. The exercise is particularly helpful when you have a perceptual problem with your brand. Fashion is a master at creating and changing perceptions in the marketplace.

It's amazing how many concrete solutions can come out pretending you're someone else. When I was overseeing the Kia Motors account, my colleagues and I imagined that Kia was a value brand like The Gap or Crate & Barrel. We visited their stores to see how those companies projected "quality for less." With those insights, and working with designer Craig Frazier, we created a dealer showroom display that looked different from any other showroom display in the car world. It consisted of light wood, soft carpet, and bright colors. Since our display was placed in the showrooms of other car companies (at first, Kia didn't have its own dealers), the design really stood out against the typical backdrop of black Plexiglas, faux marble, and plastic smiles.

Whenever you start feeling a little brand myopia coming on, take a minute, step outside your category, and get a breath of fresh ideas. It's invigorating and it can open up all kinds of areas for new partnerships, investors, customers, product lines, recruitment, and all sorts of branding opportunities. In many cases, the answers to your problems are already out there.

TWO

Core Brand Values

Before you can project a unique, external brand for your company, you must first understand the company's internal character. This internal identity—defined by the values that your company considers integral to its existence—is the source from which all other aspects of your brand, ideally, will flow.

Therefore, the first step to creating your brand roadmap will be articulating your company's core brand values. The goal is to end up with three or four values that uniquely define the essence of your company. To help you with this process, the chapter is divided into three parts. The first part will explain why core values are so important. The second part will give you some examples of core values so that you can determine which values ring true for your particular company. The third section will help you narrow your choices and help you articulate why those values are unique to your company. At the end of this chapter and the rest of the chapters in the book, you will find a worksheet, which will help you get all your thoughts down in writing.

WHY CORE VALUES ARE IMPORTANT

Without a clear set of core values, the very foundation of your brand is in jeopardy, and so is your ability to communicate your brand believably to anyone inside or outside your company. In addition, if you go too long without stating your core brand values in black and white, it's too easy to be who you're not, and that's no way to create a brand. To give you an example of why we start with core brand values, let's start with a brand that's been around for more than two hundred years—the United States of America. Suppose our forefathers had started the United States without declaring, "We hold these truths to be self-evident, that all men are created equal, that they are endowed by their Creator with certain unalienable Rights, that among these are Life, Liberty and the pursuit of Happiness."

Chances are, without the simple and clear statement of these core values, the founding of a whole new country might seem a little arbitrary and rather pointless to people. But because these values were stated so forcefully and "self-evidently," the founders of the United States were able to craft messages like the U.S. Constitution and the Bill of Rights, which have enabled the United States to keep building on its successes for more than two hundred years.

When the country went through a major crisis "fourscore and seven years" later, what did President Lincoln do? He went back to those core values. After a long-winded speech by Edward Everett, Lincoln stood up to deliver a few "wrap-up" remarks that live to this day. His first sentence states: "Fourscore and seven years ago our fathers brought forth on this continent a new nation, conceived in liberty and dedicated to the proposition that all men are created equal." Zap. Right to the core of what makes America America. All men and women are created equal, including slaves, plantation owners, Native Americans, Southerners, Northerners, Republicans, Democrats, rich, poor, and everyone in between. Never underestimate the power of core values to unite a community, a company, or a country.

Let's look at what might have happened if the founders of the United States hadn't established the nation's core values first. Suppose they had started the country by coming up with a flag first (companies generally start with their logo because they need to have letterheads, brochures, business cards, and signage). They hire this hotshot designer named Betsy Ross and ask her to design a nice flag with stars and stripes. Then they use that flag/logo to go out to the thirteen states and start talking about getting together and fighting the British. No matter how great that design was, and is, it falls short of inspiring commitment, especially a commitment with which people could possibly lose their lives, families, and property—not just market share. But once the founders committed to the core values of life, liberty, and the pursuit of happiness, suddenly the flag took on a whole new depth of meaning. It wasn't the design; it was the values the flag represented.

The same holds true for any company that wants to build on its success over the years. All the best companies have a core value system that drives all their decisions. While I was at Chiat/Day (as art director on the Apple Computer account from 1981 through 1984, through the introductions of the Apple II, Apple IIe, Apple III, Lisa, and Macintosh), Steve Jobs came to our office in San Francisco and told us about his vision to put the power of the personal computer into the hands of every person in the United States. His values were crystal clear. Everyone who worked at Apple or on the Apple account knew what the values were. Because of those values, Gary Gusick and I wrote the line "Why 1984 won't be like 1984."[1] We couldn't have come up with that idea without intimately understanding Steve Jobs's passion, and consequently Apple's, for giving power to the individual.

Disney's core values of imagination and wholesomeness have transcended changes in culture, in generations, in CEOs, and in the entertainment market. But as James Collins and Jerry Porras articulate so well in *Built to Last,* "The key point is that an enduring great company decides for itself what values it holds to be core, largely independent of the current environment, competitive requirements, or management fads."[2] Amen.

Core Values Speak Louder than Any Message

Coming up with a core set of values is even more critical in today's marketplace because we live in a marketing culture in which people have trained themselves to ferret out the superficial promises, half-truths, and overstatements. Just the sheer amount of marketing has forced people to become very selective about what they hear and what they believe. They get bombarded with thousands of messages every day, and not just from companies like your own. They get skewed and doctored messages from many of our politicians. They get heavily edited information, and sometimes misinformation, from the media. They open up their mailboxes and e-mails to find every kind of claim in the world trying to get them to act the way that particular marketer wants them to act. Our Darwinian ability to thrive and survive despite the round-the-clock saturation-spraying of marketing fertilizer is a fairly recent ability. Through our innate survival techniques, we're becoming a powerful strain of street-smart, marketing-immune, superconsumers.

You have an opportunity to penetrate that immune system by making your core values simple, believable, and unassailable. Those values will then translate into messages that are simple, believable, and unassailable in the marketplace. To accomplish this feat, you need to start within the walls of your own company.

Your Brand Is Only as Strong as Your Weakest Link

The first step to having a cohesive brand is to have a cohesive company. Core brand values can help accomplish that goal and help turn everyone in your company into a brand advocate. The person who takes reservations over the phone at Southwest Airlines is just as responsible for the brand as the pilots, maybe more so. The customers rarely interact directly with the pilots.

The same power, however, that allows your people to be an asset to your brand can also make them a liability. The credibility and integrity of your company can be undermined by just one person who doesn't understand your core values. It can happen when one employee has an inappropriate interaction with a supplier, a customer, or an investor. It can happen when a salesperson bends a few rules to make a sale. Someone in the accounting department can undermine a brand with "funny numbers."

How would you feel about the Saturn brand if you experienced a Saturn salesperson who was pushy, sexist, or dismissive? How much damage can a terse, cranky receptionist do to the image of a non-profit organization that specializes in helping people? Volvo spent thirty years becoming synonymous with safety, and then one day an executive at Volvo's ad agency said it was OK to reinforce the internal structure of a Volvo for the purpose of a television commercial.[3] The ad was supposed to be a product demonstration showing how a Volvo could withstand being driven over by a monster truck. When people found out that the demonstration was rigged, the credibility of the brand was suddenly on shaky ground. People had bought into safety's being a core value of Volvo. They bought into that value so thoroughly that they were willing to put their own lives and the lives of their children into the hands of Volvo. These same people didn't want to hear that Volvo didn't believe in its own demonstration. Consequently, because one supplier failed to understand that safety was a core value not to be tampered with, thirty years of consistent brand messaging almost went out the window. Fortunately it didn't, because Volvo does make safe cars. The marketing was flawed, not the car.

These examples show that even the best companies are vulnerable to brand damage if someone associated with the company makes a decision that's inconsistent with the company's core brand values. Because brand decisions can be made by any number of people in your company, your brand values need to be spelled out simply and clearly for everyone. Determining your own core values should help make every link in your branding chain stronger.

POTENTIAL CORE VALUES

If your company hasn't already articulated a set of core values, then it's time to figure out what they are and put them down in writing. If your company has written down a set of core values, but you feel they don't ring true to your brand, then it's time to change them or fine-tune them so that they do feel true. If your company does have a core set of values that are true mirrors of your company, then you still need to put them down in writing so that everyone in your company has access to them. Times change, employees change, marketplace conditions change. When you combine all this change with people's having to make business decisions faster and faster, you can see the necessity of having a fixed set of parameters within your decision-making process. Those are your core values. Change the core values, and you change the company. If you remove the core value of service from Nordstrom's brand, for example, you basically have just another high-end department store.

A good place to start assessing your core values is to look at the following list and check off which values represent your company. The list is compiled from a number of companies I've worked with, combined with core values listed in *America's Greatest Brands*.[4] If none of them are quite right, feel free to add some of your own. At the end of this exercise, we'll be narrowing this list down to three or four core values. Most companies that initially go through this exercise end up with about seven or eight that feel right. That's OK. You can narrow down the list later. To keep your list to a manageable number, here are a few questions to keep in the back of your head when you're looking at potential core values:

- Which values are so inherent in your company that if they disappeared, your company would cease to exist as it is?

- Which values does your company consistently adhere to in the face of all obstacles?

- Does the word *passionate* come to mind when you look at a value and apply it to your company?

- Which core values does this culture value?

We'll go into more detail later, but the preceding questions should give you a pretty good idea of what you're looking for when deciding which of the following core values best represent your company.

❏ Community
❏ Innovation
❏ Diversity
❏ Trust
❏ Irreverence
❏ Teamwork
❏ Competitiveness
❏ Connection
❏ Commitment
❏ Fun
❏ Simplicity
❏ The Golden Rule
❏ Responsiveness
❏ Pragmatism
❏ Sense of urgency
❏ Safety
❏ Integrity
❏ Quality
❏ Fairness
❏ Honesty
❏ Growth
❏ Creativity
❏ Accountability

❏ Nurturing
❏ Value
❏ Reliability
❏ Positive outlook
❏ Underpromise, overdeliver
❏ Family
❏ Entertainment
❏ Authenticity
❏ Disclosure
❏ Performance
❏ Comfort
❏ Health
❏ Education
❏ People
❏ Precision
❏ Affordability
❏ Knowledge
❏ Cleanliness
❏ Security
❏ Advanced technology
❏ Customer focus
❏ (Pick your own)

Now we'll take an in-depth look at the questions below and apply them to your potential core values.

Which Values Are So Inherent in Your Company That If They Disappeared, Your Company Would Cease to Exist as It Is?

Thousands of companies disappear every year. So why has your company survived? Why are investors still investing in your company? Why do your customers still buy your product? Why do people come to work for your company? Why do you still work for your company? These questions can help determine your company's true core values. You must be doing something right that other companies aren't doing. Or you represent something in the marketplace that other companies don't represent. Maybe you're doing it better, cheaper, faster, with more knowledgeable people, or with more efficient manufacturing. Whatever it is, you need to understand it, turn it into a core brand value, and get it working for you consistently.

A word of caution here. This is not the time to try to compensate for your company's weakness by inserting a wish list of core values currently not part of your company's identity. For example, if your success is based on your being a product-focused company, but your people skills are so-so, then admit it—that's what you are. Make the best product you can, and make sure that everyone in your company understands this passion for product quality.

If your success is based on customer service that is second to none, but your product is indiscernible from other products in the marketplace, be honest about it. You'll be happier, your employees will be happier, and you won't be creating a fantasy company in your brand roadmap. Brand roadmaps work best when they distill the true essence of a brand, as it exists, for everyone who comes in contact with the brand.

What Values Does Your Company Consistently Adhere to in the Face of All Obstacles?

The best brands do what they say they're going to do, and they do it consistently day in and day out, no matter what the circumstances. Coke doesn't have one case of soda that's so-so, another that's great, and yet another that's a bit flat. A Coke is a Coke is a Coke. It doesn't matter whether you get one at a soda fountain in Kansas City or by the Trevi Fountain in Rome. This core value, product quality, helps make Coke a great brand. When the people at Coke say they have a quality product, I believe them. There's no reason not to, even though, over the years, the company has had plenty of logistical, practical, and financial reasons not to adhere to the same standards around the world. But Coke didn't succumb to the temptation to compromise its core brand value of product quality.

A simple test to determine whether a core value is really a core value is to put it to the money test. Bill Bernbach, of the renowned ad agency Doyle Dane Bernbach, used to say, "More and more I have come to the conclusion that a principle isn't a principle until it costs you money."[5] That's especially true in this culture. Money is a reliable litmus test of whether a brand value is truly a core brand value. For example, Saturn used these words to describe itself: "Different kind of company. Different kind of car." To prove the point, it created a car company built around the customer instead of the car. The company designed friendlier dealer showrooms, hired and trained no-pressure salespeople, and installed no-haggle pricing. It didn't pad its profits by preying on the ignorance of the buyer, or "going into the back room to work out a deal." The price was the price. Whenever it had a product recall, Saturn would turn it into a community barbecue. Being a "different kind of company" cost the company a lot of money, especially initially, but it also built one of the most respected brands in the United States.

Another way to determine if a value is a core value is to see if it holds up under stressful situations, whether they be increased competition, product recall, stock devaluation, or downsizing. If your values can be downsized, they're not core values. Thomas Jefferson didn't say, "Whenever it's convenient, give me life, liberty, and the pursuit of happiness." Ford doesn't say, "Quality is Job One, Two, or Three, depending on the job." Equivocation has no role in a core brand value.

Which values in your company don't have a price tag on them? Which values hold up under all sorts of stressful circumstances? Which values can you state unequivocally? Chances are, those are your core brand values.

Does the Word *Passionate* Come to Mind When You List a Value?

Passion is a pretty foolproof test of whether a value is a core value. It will help you include your heart in the decision-making process instead of just your head. Passion is what creates an emotional connection that transcends ads, public relations, brochures, or any other crafted messages that a company puts out. To look for true brand passion, you need look no further than the most popular tattoo in the United States: the Harley-Davidson logo.[6] It's an example of a brand's being a literal brand on people's bodies.

Jerome, of Jerome's Bar-B-Que, included his passion for authentic barbecue in his brand roadmap. His definition of what it was— fall-off-the-bone, finger-lickin', mouth waterin', overnight-cooked, hardwood-smoked, open-pit barbecue—was further clarified by what it wasn't: "It definitely isn't your boil-it-and-slather-it-with-store-sauce pseudo-BBQ. You can't just zap it and wrap it like those fast food joints do and call it barbecue. That's not barbecue, that's somethin' else." Consequently, authenticity was a core brand value in Jerome's brand roadmap. His employees felt his passion; his customers could taste his passion. Authenticity was a core brand value that permeated the whole company.

Do any of the core values you listed fall into the "passionate" category? If so, then you are fortunate enough to have a core value that's automatically calling for your energy and focus.

What Core Values Does the Culture Value?

Aligning one or more of your core values with values that the culture embraces is a powerful way to motivate and connect with people. For example, Americans tend to value independence and personal expression. These values are represented by the popular icons that embody the American spirit: the blues, rock and roll, Jack Kerouac, cowboys, the Statue of Liberty, Mohammed Ali, the pioneers, Martin Luther King—the list goes on. Independence and personal expression are an integral part of American cultural values, but in Americans' day-to-day lives, these values feel as if they're missing. It could be because most Americans wear the same clothes, watch the same television programs, drive the same cars, listen to the same music, and buy the same mass-produced products. Apple is tapping into those values of independence and personal expression when it says, "Think different." With Apple, we all have the opportunity to buy a small dose of individuality. When we do, we're buying one of the core values of America as well as a product.

You can also choose a value that's intrinsic to American culture but that people somehow feel is missing. When the value is perceived as missing, people start craving that value as much, or more, than they crave a product. Nike is an example of a company's tapping into a core value that feels absent in U.S. culture. One of the critical pieces of its success has to do with "serious commitment." For almost thirty years, Nike has inspired us with athletes who have committed their lives to doing one thing and doing it extremely well—athletes like Steve Prefontaine, Joan Benoit, Carl Lewis, Michael Jordan, John McEnroe, Tiger Woods, and Mia Hamm. When we buy a Nike product, we're buying into the idea of serious commitment, whether we ever actually commit to anything or not. The idea of serious commitment is very appealing in a culture that moves from relationship to relationship, city to city, diet to diet, and job to job. So when a brand comes along that reminds us of what can happen when we actually commit to some ideal and follow through with it, then this rings true right to our physical, emotional, and spiritual core. That's a powerful motivator.

Do any of your company's core values mirror the larger core values of our culture? If they do, then leverage this advantage and you'll find that your brand resonates much deeper in people's hearts and minds.

GETTING TO THE CORE OF YOUR CORE VALUES

It's time to take your initial list of seven or eight core values and narrow that list down to three or four that will become the cornerstones of your brand. The U.S. Navy has three core values: honor, courage, and commitment.[7] Stanley Tools has four: quality, knowledge, innovation, and integrity.[8] Hush Puppies has three: fun, comfort, genuine style.[9]

The narrowing of your core values to three or four works extremely well. The fewer values you concentrate on, the more focused your company and the easier the decisions for everyone involved with your brand.

Let's put those three or four core values to an even more stringent test.

"How Can I Miss You when You Won't Go Away?"

This Dan Hicks song title is a great way to think about narrowing down your core brand values. The idea is to imagine the epitaph you would write, or your customer might write, on a tombstone if your company went out of business today (figure 2-1).

This so-called tombstone exercise is a common technique that focus-group moderators use to get people to focus on what's really

---

FIGURE 2 - 1

Tombstone Exercise

The tombstone exercise is a great way to get to the essence of your brand. List one or two qualities you would miss if your brand were gone tomorrow. Do the same with your competitors. You can also have your suppliers, employees, board of directors, and customers do this exercise. It's an effective way to see if your brand is communicating what you want it to communicate.

important with each brand. This exercise is based on the assumption that when buying our favorite brand, we don't think about how important a brand is in our lives until it's not there. The more established the brand, the more likely this will happen. If you're an Oreo cookie person, for example, how would you feel if it wasn't on the shelf the next time you went to the store? How would you feel if your favorite cereal just disappeared? Ongoing brand relationships can inadvertently become like other relationships in our lives— wife, husband, friend, and long-term employee—that get taken for granted. This exercise can help break through that "taken-for-grantedness" and help you get to the core reasons your brand exists in people's lives.

To get you started, here are some examples of potential epitaphs:

- *Nordstrom's:* I would miss their service.

- *Sony:* I would miss their incredible design and product quality.

- *Amazon.com:* I would miss their selection and value.

- *BMW:* I would miss their comfort and engineering.

You can see how a company's core brand values rise to the surface in this tombstone exercise. When you've done the exercise yourself, try it out with your suppliers, customers, and employees. It's a great way to see which values your company is effectively communicating. When you're finished, study the tombstones and see if any messages have an emotional charge to them. Do you feel warmth, sadness, nostalgia, or a smile coming on?

Which ones feel true? Which would you use as the core of your speech if you were asked to speak at that brand's funeral? We're looking for the soul of your brand. This soul exists in your core values.

Now try the same exercise with your competitors. In many cases, the emotional connections that potential customers have with your competition rise to the surface. Once you've done a set for your competitors, see if any of your values differentiate you from your competitors. Do any values set you apart from the category you're in? For example, if you have a construction company and you always deliver the job on time and on budget, then reliability and honesty are core values. Those values could very well differentiate you from all the other construction companies that will say whatever they need to say to get the job awarded to them.

Dell Computer has always had "accountability" as a core brand value. Dell is 100 percent accountable for every product it makes and every message it delivers, because it sells its computers directly to its customers. The company can't use excuses like "Why don't you take it back to the person who sold it to you?" or "Sounds like the retailer loaded in some incompatible software" or "We never promised it could do that." Dell can't pass the buck, because there's no one to pass it to. Accountability is such an ingrained part of Dell's value system, that even when Dell sold its computers through select retail outlets, it never abdicated its responsibility for its product or lost the relationship with the person who bought the computer. Accountability wasn't a value that changed when Dell briefly changed its business model.

Are Your Core Values People Oriented or Product Oriented?

Once you've collected the various epitaphs from the tombstone exercise, look them over. Do they point to your company's being people oriented or product oriented?

If you're a product-oriented company, then the epitaphs will reflect how well designed your company's products are and how much better your company's products are than any other products in the marketplace. Words like quality, consistency, reliability, attention to detail, and design expertise will rise to the top of a brand's core values. Brands like Porsche, BMW, Bosch, Sony, Braun, and Toyota are product-oriented brands and tend to have the essence of their brand defined by their products.

If you're a people-oriented company, you'll hear how wonderful it is to work at your company. Employees and suppliers will tell you how compassionate, fair, and team-oriented the management of the company is. You'll see statements that reflect superior customer relationships. People skills will be emphasized over product attributes. Brands like Nordstrom's, Southwest Airlines, and the American Red Cross represent these kinds of brands. Being a people-focused company brings a completely different set of core values to the top of the list. Words like friendly, empathetic, and unparalleled service come to represent the company's core values. This doesn't mean that Nordstrom's and Southwest Airlines don't have quality products; they do. But these companies realize that the strength of their brand, the thing that makes them different in the marketplace, is their service. This service is dependent on the talents of their people, so they're people-oriented brands. Their brand relationship is based on who they are, not what they make.

Is your company people oriented or product oriented? Pick one, and mark it on the worksheet at the end of this chapter. Knowing whether your core values are people oriented or product oriented will help you arrive at the core values that your company truly values. This knowledge will also help you when we get to the brand personality and brand icon sections of this book. People-oriented brands tend to look, feel, and sound different from product-oriented brands.

All Core Values Are Not Created Equal

As you're looking at your core values list, narrow down the list to those values that you can defend unequivocally. For example, I would consider a lot of my friends honest, but some are definitely more honest than others. For some of my friends, it's the defining aspect of who they are. When I want to avoid the truth, I generally avoid them. I would list honesty as a core value for them. For others, honesty might be one of their values, but other values may be their true strength. It doesn't mean they're not honest; it just means that there are other qualities that more uniquely define who they are. The same is true with companies. How about your company? For example, if you chose honesty as a core value, then you need to ask yourself the following questions: Are you more or less honest than your competitors? How honest are you when you learn about a possible product defect? Do you exaggerate your messages in your advertising and public relations to make a point? Are there open lines of communication within your company for both ideas and gripes? Do you tell your assistant to say you're "not in" when you are?

If honesty is a core value, then it has to permeate the whole culture of your company. Core values should live in the world of black and white, not shades of gray. When your core values are black and white, then all the people in your company understand what's expected of them and you're that much closer to doing what you say you're going to do 100 percent of the time. This means you're that much closer to being a trusted brand.

Now that you know which core values represent your company, let's add some specific descriptions that make them unique to your company.

It's Time to Get Personal

To get people to understand and buy into the core values you've listed in a brand roadmap, it helps to include with each value a paragraph explaining why that particular core value defines your company. This is especially true if someone has just joined the company and isn't sure how words like *quality, commitment,* or *fun* really position your company in the marketplace. If you leave those words up to individual interpretation, you'll get as many interpretations as you have individuals.

Here are a couple of examples from actual brand roadmaps:

- *Expertise and substance* (from Corporation for Supportive Housing): "Every message should be grounded in facts. Every solution should be actionable and relevant to the lives of our tenants. Every message should make that person or organization want to be a part of our workable, proven solution to chronic homelessness. We should be the clearinghouse for any relevant information having to do with supportive housing for the chronically homeless. Information is power in this culture. We need to have the information and wield that power to get things done."[10]

- *Inspirational and aspirational* (from A Home Away From Homelessness, a nonprofit organization in San Francisco that helps children and families in homeless situations): "People are surrounded by homelessness. On the streets. On the news. In magazines and newspapers. And it's all skewed to talking about what's not working. Our goal is to talk about what is working. We believe that people deep down in their hearts want to help. They want to believe there's a light at the beginning, middle and end of the tunnel. They want to support an organization that empowers people to go beyond their current situation and thrive. We are that organization."[11]

You get the idea. Write down your core values, and don't be afraid to express them passionately. Too many core value statements feel dispassionate. When you get stuck, specifics help. Instead of saying, "we're committed to building a better product," ask yourself what makes your product better. If you find that you're using words like *best* or *better,* ask yourself why it's "the best" or "better." Is your product more reliable? Then a core value could be reliability. Talk about why that's important to your company. Are your products better designed? Then maybe design is a core value. If it is, make me believe it. If I'm a product designer in your company, motivate me to improve every design I create for your company. If I'm a customer, make me so excited about your design that I talk about it to every person who will listen.

The one word that crops up on many core value lists is *leader.* That's not a core value. If you find yourself using the word *leader* as a core value, try to get more specific. What makes your company a leader? It usually has to do with a specific trait like honesty, compassion, reliability, or decisiveness. Those are core values that people will understand. Telling someone "I want you to be 100 percent reliable, 100 percent of the time" is a lot clearer and actionable than "I want you to be a leader." Be clear, specific, and passionate when describing your core values.

YOUR BRAND IS NOW SOLID TO THE CORE

Your brand is now based on something that won't go away. Even though the markets will change, competitors will change, financing will change, and even the rate of change will change, you have a set of core beliefs that will guide every decision you make relative to products, services, recruitment, partnerships, suppliers, business practices, and marketing opportunities. If you go no further in this book, you've succeeded. You're already ahead of the opportunistic companies that do whatever they can, and say whatever they need to say, to attract an audience and make a buck. You're light-years ahead of the companies that see their employees as numbers and their customers as open wallets.

Your Core Brand Values

If you find that the worksheets in the book don't get easier and more focused as you go along, then you might have to come back to this chapter and revisit your core values. Sometimes you get a clearer view of your values once you have to evaluate them in relation to your brand message, personality, and icons.

For example, in the initial draft of the brand roadmap for A Home Away From Homelessness, creativity wasn't listed as a core brand value. But when Jeanie Kortum, the executive director of Home Away, got to the brand personality section, she realized that art, self-expression, and creativity were an integral part of the brand. Creativity is what helps heal the kids, it inspires the teachers, and it's a powerful way for Home Away to differentiate itself in the fundraising world of other nonprofits. In the final roadmap, creativity became one of the organization's core brand values.

As you go through these worksheets, keep in mind that it's OK not to be perfect right off the bat. This is a process, not a test.

Worksheet: Your Core Brand Values

A. List eight to ten potential brand values.

1.

2.

3.

4.

5.

6.

7.

8.

9.

10.

B. Use the following questions to make sure that the values you end up with are core values.

1. Which values are so much a part of your company, that if they disappeared, your company would cease to exist as it is?

2. Are these the values that you believe your company can adhere to under stress and in the face of all obstacles?

3. Does the word *passionate* come to mind when you list a value?

C. Check one. My company is primarily
   ❏ product focused
   ❏ people focused

If you consider yourself a product company, then make sure your core values reflect that focus. The same holds true for being a people-oriented brand.

D. Now write down the three or four values that you believe are core brand values for your company. Follow each core value with a description stating why you believe each value applies specifically to your company. Doing this exercise will really help you when we come to the core message, brand personality, and brand icon sections.

1. Core value:

2. Core value:

3. Core value:

4. Core value (if necessary):

Now that you've completed this worksheet to determine your core values, we'll move on to chapter 3 to determine how your company's brand message can communicate those values.

THREE

Core Brand Message

Now that you have a set of core brand values, the next step is to create a core brand message that communicates the essence of your brand. The core brand message is the key message that your company will be communicating to all its audiences. All other messages coming from your company will be offshoots of this message. This chapter will take you through a process that will ensure that the brand message you come up with will work in the marketplace for years to come.

WHY DOES YOUR COMPANY EXIST IN THE MARKETPLACE?

The more closely your core message reflects the reality of your brand and why it exists, the more effective your brand message will be—both within your company and to the outside world. For example, some companies exist because they're the only ones that make a specific product. Sometimes you're all alone in the marketplace because the category grew so fast that the cost of entry into that category became too prohibitive for new competitors to enter and succeed. If you have a unique position or product in the marketplace, then writing a core message is pretty easy. State what you do in the most inspirational way possible, and then move on to determine your brand personality.

If you don't have a unique position, then you'll need to work a little harder at crafting a core message. If it isn't obvious why you exist in the marketplace, then there are other ways to arrive at a core message that will work.

SEPARATING PERCEPTION FROM REALITY

Branding can be challenging for many reasons, some of which are perceptual, and some of which are integral problems with the product or service you offer. It's easier to fix or strengthen a brand when there's a perceptual problem—a communication breakdown or a misunderstanding—than if there's a serious internal problem, such as a defective product, poor distribution, or nonexistent service. If you run into a serious internal problem, you'll need to correct that problem before you focus your resources and marketing materials on branding. To get a quick snapshot of the areas your company needs to address, prepare a two-column list with "perception" written on one side and "reality" on the other. When filling it out, be as objective as possible so that the list provides the insights you need to create an effective roadmap. Consider, for example, the list created for The Branson School, a private high school in a rich, white, and fairly exclusive neighborhood. Over the years, the perception of Branson mirrored the neighborhood it was in, despite the fact that the reality was quite different.

PERCEPTION	REALITY
White	Ethnic mix
Uniform thinking	Diverse thinking, diverse subjects
Elitist	Inclusive
Cool	Passionate
Isolated	Community focused
Impersonal	Personal
Cookie-cutter kids	Individualistic kids
Intelligent	Intelligent
Only wealthy	20 percent on financial aid

Coming up with this list really helped the school develop a powerful core brand message that reinforced the reality of what was going on at the school.

Once you've finished the perception-versus-reality exercise, you should be a little closer to the real issues that need to be addressed with your marketing. With this reality fresh in your mind, you can then begin to look at the big picture and get a feeling for which ideas, already in our culture, you could use to help solve your branding issues.

HOW TO COME UP WITH A BIG IDEA

One of the big challenges of creating a core brand message is making sure it will be as valid in five or ten years as it is today. To come up with a timeless message, you'll need to take a few steps back to gain perspective. Start by stepping away from your day-to-day business. Then take a few more steps back until the category you're in disappears. Then take a few more steps back until the whole business world disappears. Finally, step back until you can see the cultural horizon and spot which landmarks are a constant part of that land-scape. For example, the pioneer spirit is an integral part of the American cultural landscape. The United States was established by pioneers, whose spirit didn't stop with Plymouth Rock, Ellis Island, the gold rush, or even Silicon Valley. Americans are obsessed with new horizons in commercial products, art, music, technology, business, and all other facets of their lives. As a culture, Americans are always looking for new information, new perspectives, and new answers to all kinds of problems. It's the reason so many people from around the world flock to the United States and why this nation has so many entrepreneurs, patents, and opportunities to succeed. The pioneer spirit is something you can tap into as a company, which can lead to powerful core ideas like these:

- Constant improvement (Avis: "We try harder")

- Tenacity (Timex: "It takes a licking and keeps on ticking")

- Individual betterment (U.S. Army: "Be all you can be")

- Perseverance (Citibank: "The Citi never sleeps")

It's important to look at the overall values that motivate the culture to which you're marketing and to identify those that have existed for at least twenty to thirty years. Otherwise, you might get mired in today's news and last week's trends. Stepping away from your day-to-day reality will help you come up with a message that won't be obsolete in a year or two.

HOW TO CRAFT YOUR CORE BRAND MESSAGE

You have analyzed why your brand exists in the marketplace, clari-fied your perception-versus-reality issues, studied various cultural

When you're creating a core message, it helps to have as many different per-spectives as possible. Think in terms of triangulating a location. If you have only one point of reference, that's the least accurate way to hone in on an exact position. If you can introduce two points of reference, your positioning becomes that much more accurate. When you can have three different points of reference, you can accurately arrive at the epicenter of your positioning. When you have more than three angles, you're definitely in the fine-tuning mode. Once you come up with a core message that you feel positions your company, consider running it by your customers or someone in another department. Getting as many points of reference as possible can help create a more accurate message.

value checkpoints, and pinpointed your positioning. Now you're ready to turn that knowledge into a single sentence that will become your core brand message.

"When all else fails, simplify." This thought, which my creative director Lee Clow embraced and passed on to me and others, was a mantra throughout my years in advertising. As a result, people didn't have to navigate through my confusion to find out what I was trying to say. A look at many company mission statements suggests that most companies could heed this advice as well. Let's take a closer look at the steps you can take to make sure your core brand message is as simple and effective as it can be. In crafting your mes-sage, you need to answer the following questions:

- Is your core message simple and clear enough?

- Does it differentiate you in the marketplace?

- Is it true?

• Is it relevant?

• Is it consistent with your company's core brand values?

• Can you be the first to say it?

Is Your Core Message Simple and Clear Enough?

Al Ries and Jack Trout observed more than twenty years ago in their best-seller *Positioning: A Battle for Your Mind:* "The best approach to take in our overcommunicated society is the oversimplified message."[1] Here's a simple exercise to see if the core brand message you come up with is oversimplified: Read it to someone, and ask the listener to repeat it back. If he or she can't, it's not simple enough. If the listener can repeat it back, go back to the person ten minutes later to see if he or she can still repeat it back. Remember, this is the core message that all your marketing decisions will be executed against. If it doesn't pass a simple, repeatable test within your company, chances are slim to none that it will survive the revolving door of marketing directors, ad agencies, design firms, public relations firms, Web site designers, event planners, product designers, salespeople, and everyone else who represents your brand in the marketplace.

Does Your Core Message Differentiate You in the Marketplace?

The goal of reading your core message to others is to make sure it positions your company uniquely in the marketplace, rather than conjuring up the names of other companies that exist in your category. The worst-case scenario is discovering that you spent your time and money communicating a brand message but your audience walks away remembering your competition. This can happen if your brand message is too close to a competitor's message, if your competitor is outspending you, or if your core message is generic to the category and there are larger, better-known companies in that category. If you can create a brand message that clearly separates you from your major competitors, you'll be that much further ahead when it comes to getting a customer to commit to your brand (figure 3-1).

Is Your Core Message True?

Believability is the biggest hurdle any company has to overcome when it creates a core brand message. To protect your company against unbelievable claims, read the brand message to someone, and see if it's believable to him or her. If it isn't believable to you or to the people within your company, how can you expect it to be believable to anyone else? In the creation of a core message, the best place to start is with irrefutable facts. For instance, the old slogan of Federal Express, "When it absolutely, positively has to be there

FIGURE 3 - 1

Customer Commitment

Which choice is easier to make? Think about it, because the same decisions occur in branding. If you're asking a consumer to choose between shades of gray, not only is the decision harder to make, but the consumer feels less committed to the decision. The more polarized you make the choice, the better chance you have that a customer will commit to your brand.

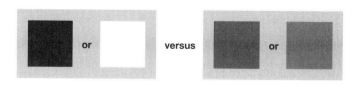

overnight," is a fact. "Seriously committed athletes wear Nikes" is a fact. "7-Up: The Uncola" is a fact. Some of the most emotionally persuasive brands have messages based on a strong fact. Apple's "Think different" campaign is based on a number of facts. Apple creates products that look different, it has a computer operating system that's different from its competitors' systems, it advertises differently, and it talks to its customers differently. "Think different" is not simply a tag line; it's a core value and a core message captured in two words. Because of its commitment to that message and set of values, Apple has created a very strong emotional connection with its customers. Which facts lay the foundation that you could use for your brand message?

Is Your Core Message Relevant?

Make sure your message is relevant to the people you want to reach. Otherwise, your message will disappear into thin air. How many car commercials do you remember when you're not in the market for a car?

Relevance may seem like an obvious checkpoint for a core message, but it isn't for a lot of companies. Many companies use their brand message to blow their own narcissistic horns, telling people, "We're the fastest-growing this," "We're the most-trusted that," or "We're the world's best this." Unfortunately, no one generally cares outside the walls of that particular company. Most people want to know what's in it for them. They want to believe that a company's message speaks directly to them and not just to the company's ego.

Relevance is also good for the bottom line. Howard Gossage, a member of the Copywriter's Hall of Fame and a true genius of marketing, stated it this way in *Is There Any Hope for Advertising?* "If you have something pertinent to say you neither have to say it to very many people—only to those who you think will be interested—nor do you have to say it very often. How many times do you have to be told that your house is on fire? How often does your wife have to read that a coat she has been lusting for has been reduced from $200 to $79.50 before she is off and running? How often do you have to read a book, a news story, or see a movie or play? If it is interesting, once is enough; if it is dull, once is plenty."[2]

Gossage's point of view is so refreshing in a culture where marketers believe repetition is the key to memorability. Where marketers believe repetition is the key to memorability. Where marketers believe repetition is . . . The key to memorability is relevance. The key to annoying people is mindless repetition.

Is Your Core Message Consistent with the Core Values of Your Company?

Your core message is usually delivered at the point at which you're letting people know who you are, and they're basing the beginnings of a brand relationship on that knowledge. It's critical that your core values line up with the key message that your company will be communicating to those people. As with any relationship, if what you're communicating isn't really who you are, then your brand is in jeopardy.

If you're having a problem distilling your core message down to a simple sentence, imagine you're at a party and someone asks you about your company. What one sentence would you use to describe your company? Or think about a prospect who's interviewing with your company and wants a simple "handle" that will help him or her differentiate you from other companies in your category. Looking at the core message this way sometimes helps keep your core message a little more conversational and will also keep you from creating the world's longest run-on sentence.

Can You Be the First to Say Your Core Message?

Many valid messages get eliminated because someone says, "Wait, our competitor can say that, too." The concern should not be with what your competitors can theoretically say, but which message you can actually own. When Federal Express advertised, "When it absolutely, positively has to be there overnight," it wasn't the only company able to deliver on this promise. Emery Express, Airborne Express, and even the U.S. Post Office could do it. But Federal Express focused its brand on this one message, and the company owned it. More importantly, FedEx made people believe it. The brand became synonymous with guaranteed overnight delivery.

The first company to state its message simply and clearly usually owns the message. The first one to say it and get its customers to believe it through personal experience has a great shot at owning this message. In a culture that remembers winners and tends to forget the runners-up, being first is a huge advantage. Is there any message that you can own if you say it first in the marketplace?

If You're Stuck, Steal from the Best

To get the ideas flowing, it's always helpful to begin by looking at advertising slogans like "Maxwell House: Good to the last drop." The best ones condense a complicated thought into a few words. Because of that simplicity and discipline, they're worth studying.

Core brand message. Slogans. Headlines. Those terms can get confusing when you are trying to develop a core brand message, but they're actually distinct entities.

The core brand message is the core idea that later gets expressed by slogans and headlines. Slogans and headlines are the children of the parent idea: the core brand message.

A slogan, also known as a tag line—because it's usually "tagged" onto the end of a television commercial or the end of a print ad—is the line that generally sits near the logo. Sometimes it mirrors the core brand message, as in the case of General Electric's "We bring good things to life." But many times it doesn't. "Do you Yahoo!" is a call to action, not a core brand message. The same goes for the American Express tag line "Don't leave home without it" and Nike's "Just do it."

The headline is generally what goes at the top of an ad. It's the encapsulation of whatever message the company is trying to deliver that day. It tends to be more of a tactical message. In GE's case, it could be the announcement of a new dishwasher. Or in Visa's case, the message could be a new promotional offer or a new credit card rate. A company can deliver hundreds of different headlines to the marketplace every year. Headlines change; slogans generally don't. And core messages never should.

A good place to check out the world's best slogans is the Advertising Slogan Hall of Fame (http://www.adslogans.co.uk). The Web site lists the twenty-five greatest slogans of all time, as well as the current slogans of the top one hundred global brands (according to *Business Week/Interbrand*). Many of the most effective slogans incorporate the key brand message, like "We try harder" and "The Ultimate Driving Machine." Without seeing the company names, you probably still knew exactly which companies created the preceding slogans and what they stood for. That's potent. It also didn't take a paragraph or two to communicate the essence of the brand. In most cases, the most memorable slogans are only three to five words long.

You can also study other companies' messages by going to their Web site or reading through their annual report. For example, if you go the American Red Cross Web site (http://www.redcross.org), you'll see their crystal clear message in the upper left-hand corner of their home page: Together we can save a life. Those few words are relevant, differentiating, inclusive, compelling, and totally consistent with their core brand values.

TRANSFERRING YOUR MESSAGE INTO PEOPLE'S LONG-TERM MEMORY

Narrowing your core brand message to three to five words is a tough order, but it's worth striving for. That kind of simplicity and clarity will help people remember your brand, not just in their short-term memory, but also in their long-term memory.

Understanding how memory works is key to constructing your core message. Long-term memory is where brands live, and short-term memory is where brands visit. Although the following information is oversimplified, it helps you determine whether you've created a brand message that will become lodged in people's long-term memory.

Short-Term Memory Is Information That's Meant to Be Discarded

When you're driving down the road, short-term memory analyzes the car coming at you, its speed, whether it's swerving or not, and so forth. As soon as it passes, the information is discarded. The same holds true for most marketing materials. Most such material is meant to get immediate results, but it's not information that the customers feel they need to hang on to. For example, a sale on a specific product today is information that consumers know they don't have to store in long-term memory, because that information will be obsolete in a day, a week, or a month.

You can see the results of this discarded information in the company's ledger pad: Run a lease ad, see a sales spike. Drop some coupons in the Sunday paper, see a sales spike. Announce free bagels, see a sales spike. There's usually no residual effect, however, for the dollars spent. Most marketing falls into this "discarded" category. How many messages do you remember from today's newspaper ads? If you can help it, you don't want your brand message to be in the "discarded" category.

Long-Term Memory Is Information That's Meant to Be Stored

Any information that contributes to a person's physical and emotional well-being gets stored in long-term memory. This is where you want your brand to live. This is where simplicity and clarity can help.

Why the need for simplicity and clarity? We need them because long-term memory doesn't store information in its entirety. As Steven Pinker articulates in *How the Mind Works,* the connected structures "which put memories into long-term storage . . . carry what neuroscientists call 'highly processed' input coming from regions one or more stops downstream from the first sensory areas."[3] In other words, the mind simplifies and stereotypes information coming from your initial input.[4] It then stores that information with other simplified, stereotyped information. In a general sense, cars get stored with cars, and fast-food restaurants get stored with other fast-food restaurants. In a specific sense, Sony thoughts get stored with Sony thoughts.

By presimplifying your company's brand message, you can "send" your message directly into the consumer's long-term memory and to the place you want it stored. Once the message is lodged there, it's very hard to change that perception. The mind is stubborn that way; it likes to reinforce its views, not change them. That's good news for brands that have missteps along the way. For example, when someone found a syringe in a can of Pepsi, the incident could have destroyed a lot of brands. But because our long-term memory wants to reinforce our belief that Pepsi is a safe, trusted brand, we were willing to listen to Pepsi and dismiss the event as an anomaly. People's tenacity to hang onto long-held beliefs in the face of bad news holds true with all the established brands, whether it's the Ford and Firestone tires mishap or the Tylenol scare.

Another advantage of having your core message lodged in the customer's long-term memory is that you're able to add emotional depth and new information to that "stereotyped" information. It's like someone you've known for twenty years. Once you've established a relationship, every new piece of information adds depth and interest to that relationship. Your image of an old friend has a lot more subtleties and is less simplistic and stereotypical than your image of someone you've just met. Great brands understand this.

If your brand doesn't have a simple core idea lodged in the consumer's mind, then there might not be anything for your other messages to latch onto. If that's the case, then in all likelihood, your future messages will turn into short-term, discarded information.

Nike's clothes campaign of the 1980s is a perfect example of how powerful a brand can be when it's securely lodged in long-term memory. The Chiat/Day creative team of Gary Johns and Jeff Gorman immersed themselves in all the data about their target, the market, the competition, the product, and the target's aspirations. The team simplified the Nike message down to two simple visuals: (1) a picture of a famous athlete in sweaty Nike clothes after a strenuous workout and (2) a Nike clothes tag hanging from the edge of the ad.

When customers were shown the ads, the amount of information communicated by those two visuals was incredible. People said the clothing was durable, nonchafing, easy to clean, stylish, well made, light, comfortable, contemporary, uniquely designed, practical, colorfast, and a good value. Not a bad list of product attributes for an ad without a word of copy. It won the Stephen E. Kelly Award for best print campaign of the year.

Understanding what's already in the long-term memory of your audience can make your branding job a whole lot easier.

Also bear in mind that if you don't simplify your core message, the mind will, and you might not like what other people's minds come up with, or where the message gets stored.

To test the importance of long-term memory on branding, cut out the logo of a well-known brand—Wal-Mart, Toyota, Tiffany, Sony, United Way—and write down all the thoughts, words, and values that you associate with that brand. Then try it with your main competitor's logo. Finally, try it with your own logo. This exercise can help you determine what to say, and more importantly, what you don't have to say, because the information is already there in the customer's long-term memory.

CREATING THE RIGHT MESSAGE FOR YOUR AUDIENCE

Now that you've looked at why your brand exists in the marketplace, separated the perceptual issues from the real ones, and acquired some tools to find a big idea and craft it into a core brand message, you need to find the people who will be passionate about that message. Let's say that you've got a core brand message that you feel really good about, and the people in your company love it too. It's time to look at how the key people outside of your company see, hear, and react to your message. These people will be called your lightning-rod target.

Mapping and Zapping Your Lightning-Rod Target

The term *lightning-rod target* came from the marketing people at Boston Market. Boston Market defined its lightning-rod target as the one person who felt passionately about the company's core brand message. In Boston Market's case, the message was home-style meals. Once the target was determined, all the company's marketing messages were directed at that one person. This person was determined by his or her passion, not the volume potential. Most companies determine their target by the potential sales volume of a particular segment. In many cases, however, the lightning-rod target is not a huge market, but can affect a huge market and drive a lot of sales.

Sometimes the lightning-rod targets are the people we call experts. Nike gets buy-in from the sports "experts"—successful coaches and athletes—who then influence others to wear Nike shoes and apparel. An expert can also be the neighborhood grease monkey whom the neighbors go to for car information and recommendations. Experts can be extremely influential in getting someone to try a brand.

Sometimes the lightning-rod target is a person known as a *gatekeeper* to the brand. In the case of Boston Market's Kids Program, mom was the gatekeeper. She, and not the kid, became the lightning-rod target. Even though Boston Market was selling kids meals, mom was the passionate one about giving her kids home-style meals. The kids couldn't care less. Whatever came with a toy and tasted all right was fine with them. Because she was the portal to the brand, Boston Market crafted its core message with her as the audience.

Given the realities of your product and your situation, who do you believe your lightning-rod target is? Who is the one person who will look at your core message and take it to heart? Who will tell all her friends about your company? Who will willingly put himself on your mailing list? Who will look for you and your products without your always having to initiate the contact? To build a truly powerful brand, the brand relationship needs some sort of proactive approach from both parties. To start that interaction, talk to your customers about your values. If you respect the customers, or value their input, let them know. Your lightning-rod target should be your top priority. With that in mind, write down who your lightning-rod target is, and then see if you're solving a real problem in that target's mind. If you go through this exercise, you're a few steps closer to creating a trusted brand.

Making Sure That What You Say Is What They Hear

Once you understand the needs of your lightning-rod target and can truthfully deliver on those needs, you'll probably want to have some ways of making sure your brand message is communicating what you want it to communicate. Two approaches are fairly common in marketing circles: focus-group testing and copy testing. If you're interested in pursuing either of these directions, various books on the subject—both pro and con—can help you. My favorite is Jon Steel's *Truth, Lies and Advertising,* a fair, informative, and entertaining book grounded in his own personal experiences with some of the best-thought-out, best-executed, and best-liked campaigns in the United States.[5] The campaigns include Polaroid, "Got Milk," E*Trade, Foster Farms, and Hewlett-Packard, to name a few.

There are varying opinions on the effectiveness of focus-group and copy testing, and a multitude of variations within each type of testing. The enormous amount of details involved with these two approaches lies outside the scope of this book. It is important, however, to have an overview of both approaches.

In their simplest form, the two types of feedback fall into the categories of either qualitative or quantitative testing. *Qualitative testing* involves some sort of interaction between a moderator and another person or a group. The interaction can take place in focus groups (six to ten individuals who are gathered together and then asked questions about various communication issues), minigroups, one-on-one interviews, person-on-the-street interviews, mall intercepts, telephone interviews, and on-line interviews. The advantage of qualitative testing is that a moderator can probe issues, follow up on concerns, encourage ideas, and use the personal interaction to get below the surface of initial reactions or answers. For the purpose of creating a brand message, interactive qualitative testing will probably give you more usable information than will quantitative testing.

Quantitative testing is meant to turn reactions into raw data. Because of that, this testing tends to be less intuitive and more scientific than focus-group testing. In a quantitative communication test, people are shown concepts, in the form of a television commercial, storyboard, or print ad and are then asked to fill out forms based on various criteria and sliding scales of interest, persuasion, and likability. Clients who are looking for hard numbers and percentages to validate or invalidate people's reactions generally gravitate toward copy testing.

Because of these differences, qualitative testing is generally used at the initial stages of an idea, when a company is exploring ideas, opinions, reactions, and the impact of various messages. Quantitative testing is generally used at the end of the process, when a company knows what it wants to say and who it wants to say it to. In this situation, a company can quantitatively measure specific reactions to predict the reactions of the greater population.

Both of these approaches have their strengths and weaknesses. Before committing to either one, you should explore the differences in more depth. Numerous marketing books discuss the various testing methods; you can also check out the Web sites of the myriad research firms on the Internet.

Tapping into the "People-ness" of People

If you have the time and the resources, the most useful and informative communication check is to talk to a person in his or her own environment. It's amazing what you can find out. You can get a sense of who people are, what they love, what they read, what music they listen to, and how chaotic or organized their life is. There's no substitution for direct experience and direct contact with your audience.

To discover the "teenager-ness" of teenagers, interview them at their favorite hangout. It could be at their home, local community center, skateboard park, outdoor concert, or high school sports event. To experience the mom-ness of moms, spend time with them between five and seven o'clock at night, when they're juggling dinner, catching up on phone messages, monitoring homework, and chauffeuring their kids to and from after-school activities. What you're looking for is the people-ness of people in their environments. I haven't been able to find any of that "wonderfulness" in the one-way, mirrored rooms of focus-group facilities or the data-filled pages of copy testing. There are certain communication issues that you'll only discover by being out with your audience in the real world. It's a great way to see how your brand fits into the rest of a person's life. The experience keeps your brand message well grounded.

PROTECTING YOUR MESSAGE

Now that you've found your lightning-rod target and crafted a message that's compelling to him or her, let's see if that message can be owned and defended out in the marketplace. Sometimes you can come up with a core brand message that really works for your company, but there are a number of reasons you can't own it in the marketplace. Some of the more common reasons include the following:

1. *A bigger or more popular brand already owns that message.* The number one and two leading brands in any category usually own the number one and two reasons that people buy the product or service (e.g., Coke and Pepsi, Hertz and Avis, Duracell and Energizer). If you find your brand in that third, fourth, or fifth position, you'll need to find a message that differentiates you from those competitors. If you don't, and you

end up communicating the same core message that they do, people will react to *your* message by going to *their* brands. In terms of numbers, if numbers one and two own 90 percent of the market and you own 10 percent, nine out of ten people who hear your message will buy their product.

2. *The message isn't believable coming from your company.* Sometimes it takes time for a brand to build credibility within a market. In the early to mid-1990s, Dell was in this position with its servers. Despite Dell's reputation for reliable notebooks and personal computers, many companies weren't willing to put their mission-critical applications onto Dell servers. Dell was viewed as strictly a PC company; consequently, customers gravitated to the more established companies in the category: Compaq and IBM. This customer preference changed, but it took time.

3. *The message requires too much education to be easily understood by potential customers.* Intelligy was a whole new educational system for kids, but required way too much education to be appreciated. The system was such an experiential set of products that the company ended up selling the products at local meetings at people's houses to give prospects the time and the opportunity to experience the product for themselves. When your message is so complicated or layered that it can't be described in ten words or less, then you might want to resort to the solution proposed by Nicholas Samstag: "It is, in fact, a lot easier to seduce a person than to transfer information to him. . . . [P]eople resist being instructed while they do not resist being amused and charmed and teased. What is more, true instruction takes time and money. To educate a

prospect (or, harder still, to re-educate him) is a long-term effort, often too expensive to be worth it."[6]

4. *The message is too new in the culture and requires time and other businesses to validate the category, product, or message.* When I first started working on the Apple II, people had no idea what a personal computer could do for them. So before we could sell the computer, we needed to sell the idea of personal computing. As a result, Apple spent a lot of its marketing dollars talking about word processing, database management, e-mail, business graphics, and other mainstream business applications. In essence, Apple was selling the software and not the hardware. Once IBM came into the PC category with its Charlie Chaplin commercials, it validated the category and enabled Apple to go back to selling what really made Apple distinctive: its easy-to-use operating system and its products.

5. *Something happened previously to another brand that rubs off on your brand.* For example, Kia's being the second Korean car company in the United States after the travails of Hyundai in the late 1980s and early 1990s made us at Goldberg Moser O'Neill much more conscious of what messages Kia could own, and which ones it couldn't.

After you've taken some of these issues into consideration and determined which message you clearly *cannot* own in the marketplace, you'll want to make sure that the message that you *can* own is effectively defensible over the life of your brand. For example, if your core message introduces larger companies into your competitive set, then you'll need to increase your marketing dollars to make sure your message is effectively seen and heard. If you don't have the dollars, people, or resources to compete effectively, then you need to either refocus your message more narrowly or find another message that won't demand those resources.

THE BULL'S-EYE EXERCISE

The bull's-eye exercise can give you a good indication of who your competition is and whether you have the resources necessary to defend your core message against that competition. In this exercise, a series of concentric circles helps you visualize the strengths and weaknesses of your message in the greater world of marketing (figure 3-2). It's a particularly good exercise for determining whether your core message is specific enough to be owned.

For example, when I was collaborating with my clients at Near Bridge Consulting, we used the bull's-eye exercise to help position it in the marketplace. Near Bridge Consulting was a start-up company that specialized in predicting trends six to eighteen months out. It also supplied training, in-depth research, and general business consulting. To get started, we had the company write "near-term trend experts" in the inner circle. In other words, Near Bridge's core message was its expertise in near-term trends. As part of the exercise, we wanted to see who else owned, or could own, that specific positioning. We couldn't think of anyone else with this expertise.

We moved out to the next circle and wrote "long-term trend experts." McKinsey & Company, Bain & Company, and some other very formidable competitors suddenly appeared on our chart.

Then we went out to the third circle from the center and listed "training." In addition to McKinsey and Bain, other major competitors

FIGURE 3 - 2

Bull's-eye Exercise?

The bull's-eye exercise is one way to estimate how expensive it will be to own more than one message in the marketplace. For every message you add to your core message (+1, +2, or +3), you add competitors and marketing dollars. For example, if you're a restaurant that specializes in steak, make that your core message. List the competitors that stand for steak. If you also want to highlight your seafood, move out a ring and make your core message "steak + seafood." Now list all the new competitors that offer steak only; both steak and seafood; and seafood only (you're competing with them now, too). If you also want to highlight your chicken dishes, move out another ring (steak + seafood + chicken), and add all the competitors that have steak only; seafood only; chicken only; steak and seafood; steak and chicken; chicken and seafood; and steak, chicken, and seafood. The permutations become mind-boggling. Not only does every additional message add marketing dollars and competitors, but it also dilutes your core message so that someone else can come in and own it. Giving up real estate in your audience's mind is a very costly proposition.

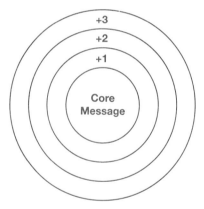

appeared. We decided not to go out any further, because the further we got away from what was unique about Near Bridge's brand, the more we introduced issues and competitors that could crush a start-up like Near Bridge. The enormous cost of entry to compete with those kinds of competitors wouldn't be feasible, let alone profitable.

To better understand where you stand in relation to your competitors, create your own series of concentric circles, and put your core message in the middle circle. As you start moving outward with broader messages, start adding competitors and dollars. You'll soon discover, given the resources of your company and the competitors you're facing, where you'll want to focus your message and dollars.

WORKSHEET

Your Core Brand Message

Going through the questions on this worksheet will help ensure that your core brand message is as powerful and differentiating as it can be.

A. Why does your brand exist? (Write one or two sentences.)

B. How is your brand perceived in the marketplace? (Write down an overall impression.)

C. List five perceptions of your brand in the marketplace versus the reality.

PERCEPTION   REALITY

1.

2.

Worksheet: Your Core Brand Message

PERCEPTION   REALITY

3.

4.

5.

D. Are there any cultural trends that your brand can leverage? (List two or three.)

1.

2.

3.

E. What is your core brand message (in fifteen words or less)?

F. Can you give an unqualified yes to the following questions about your core brand message?

1. Is your message as simple and clear as you can make it?

2. Does it differentiate you in the marketplace?

3. Is it true?

4. Is it relevant?

5. Is it consistent with your company's core values?

G. Who is the lightning-rod target for this message?

H. What makes this message relevant to that target? (Write a sentence or two.)

I. What are the key support points that make your message believable to your lightning-rod target?

J. Is your message safe in the marketplace, according to the bull's-eye exercise? Why? (Write a few sentences that state why you're uniquely able to own and defend your message.)

K. What impression do you want your various audiences to take away from your core brand message? (State it in the words of the customer. For example, for Paul Newman's Salad Dressing brand, I might say, "Finally, there's a quality consumer product that's good for me and good for others.")

L. If you're a people-oriented company, is your core message people oriented? If you're a product-oriented company, is your core message product oriented?

Now you're ready to go on to the next chapter, where you'll determine what personality traits you'll use to engage people with your brand.

FOUR

Brand Personality

In this chapter, we'll determine the personality that your brand is going to use to communicate your core values and core message. Defining that tone and attitude will make it easier to keep all your communications on target. This defined personality can create an immediate point of differentiation in the marketplace: David Aaker takes that thought one step further and states: "The important aspect of a brand personality is that it is often a sustainable point of differentiation. Consider the personalities of Harley-Davidson, Saturn, Hallmark, Tiffany, Obsession (by Calvin Klein), Jack Daniel's, United Airlines, or Mercedes-Benz. In each case, the brand personality is unique within the product class."[1]

WHAT DO WE MEAN BY BRAND PERSONALITY?

Every company has a personality. It's impossible for a company not to have a personality, just as it's impossible for a person not to have a personality. Even "zero" personality is a personality.

Many companies inadvertently fall into that "zero" personality trap. The two most common reasons are (1) because too many people within the organization are determining the personality and (2) because no one is doing so. In the first case, when a company hasn't defined or committed to a brand personality, every piece of communication takes on the personality of the person doing that particular communication. As a result, the brand personality becomes a mishmash of various traits, and a clearly defined personality disappears. In the second case, companies avoid defining a personality, because they want to be seen as objective. In this case, they err on the side of presenting fact after fact in their marketing materials. What they don't realize is that a customer views them the same way that a customer would view a salesperson who refused to interact with the potential prospect and merely dropped off a product fact sheet and walked out the door. Even if the sale is made, there is no emotional contact and a major opportunity has been missed. As soon as someone comes in with the same facts, but delivers those facts with an engaging personality, the first salesperson has lost a customer and a sale.

There is no neutral ground. If your personality is ill defined, you're vulnerable to other brands with defined personalities. If your personality isn't engaging people, you're losing them. This chapter will help you determine which personality traits will engage your audiences. We're looking for consistency and appropriateness *for your company*. We're looking for personality traits that will consistently show up from the top of your company to the bottom, from the memo pads on your desks to your annual report. Healthy brands, like healthy relationships, aren't created with multiple and inconsistent personalities. David Ogilvy, author of the classic *Confessions of an Advertising Man*, put it this way: "The manufacturer who dedicates his advertising to building the most sharply defined personality for his brand will get the largest share of the market at the highest profit."[2]

THE COMMON PITFALLS OF CREATING A BRAND PERSONALITY

Before you develop your sharply defined brand personality, consider some of the common mistakes that companies make when they start listing personality traits. Understanding some common problems is useful, because most companies are relatively experienced at determining what they want to say, but not necessarily how they want to say it. Most companies are fairly comfortable going through the core values and core message exercises because they've already had a lot of personal experience crafting mission statements, strategy documents, positioning statements, quarterly objectives, and competitive analyses. They're generally not as comfortable when they have to write down their brand personality, a responsibility usually delegated to their marketing people, ad agencies, speech writers, design firms, public relations firms, and Web site designers. The delegating can be a problem itself. So can other practices that companies follow when they try to create a brand personality. Let's look at these pitfalls individually.

Delegating the Brand Personality to Someone Outside the Company

Your brand personality should be an accurate representation of your company; otherwise, you're creating a brand relationship that's based on someone else's personality. You would be acting like a modern-day Cyrano de Bergerac—reflecting the passions of your company through someone else's prism. Abdicating direct responsibility for your brand personality is a dangerous game to play, because customers don't go out and buy the ad agency, designer, writer, consultant, or public relations firm; they buy your product or service. They buy your company and what it represents. If your company doesn't quite live up to the "sizzle" of the marketing, then your relationship with the customers is in jeopardy. Suddenly the customers realize that they bought the technique and not the substance.

It's not my goal to eliminate the role of ad agencies, design firms, or brand consultants, but their role needs to be carefully defined. Outside agencies and consultants can bring their unique talents and a certain objectivity to the process of helping you create a brand personality, but the personality needs to be yours, not theirs.

Changing Personality Whenever There's a Change in Audiences or Messages

Placing too much emphasis on the audience is another misconception that's rampant in the United States. You see it all the time with the politicians who rely on polls to tell them who they are and how they should relate to people. It happens with companies, too. They "read their audience" and turn themselves into what they think the audience wants. They become personality chameleons. When they want to talk to young people, they create a personality that's rowdy, loud, and antiestablishment. When they decide to go after the over-sixty crowd, they become quiet, thoughtful, and traditional.

A word of advice: Don't. Your brand personality should be who you are in all circumstances. This gets back to having a solid idea of who you are and making sure that every external expression of it is consistent with this identity. That's how relationships and trust are built. That's how brands are built.

Misjudging the Balance of What Is Said versus How It Is Said

The United States represents a culture that's enamored with "the newest this" and "the newest that." This craving for "the latest and the greatest" leads many companies down the ultrarational road of touting the infinitesimal differences in their products and services. But frankly, after twenty-plus years in the advertising business working with some of the most innovative companies in the world, I have learned that most product differences aren't remarkable enough to base a brand upon. Companies have become so adept at copying products and services that "newness" becomes only a short-term tactic for creating awareness and driving sales. This is most obvious in the technology category, but it spans many product categories. If a company comes out with an XYZ-megahertz computer this week, then five more companies will have the same computer next week. If Hertz introduces a new service, you can bet that Avis, Budget, and National will not be far behind.

To make the point even clearer, let's look at a truly innovative idea: electric cars. Electric vehicles represent a powerful, rational difference in the car industry, but who's been able to build a brand on that fact? Who was first? Who owns "electric car" in the minds of the American audience? No one has, even though many companies advertise that they make electric cars. Building an electric car has become a powerful way for companies like Saturn, Honda, and Toyota to reinforce their brand perception of being innovative companies, but the car itself hasn't created enough electricity, so to speak, to separate one brand from another.

Because people are bombarded with so much new, and sometimes conflicting, claims each day, how you say the information is critical. A helpful exercise is to assume that every rational point you could possibly make is exactly the same as the competitions' points. When you set aside all the rational reasons to buy your product or service, emotional reasons start to emerge. That's where your true brand personality lives—in the emotional realm. Once you've captured the emotional reasons for people's buying, then the rational reasons become powerful ways to close the sale.

There's also a practical reason to set aside the rational reasons to buy your product or service. As a brand grows and matures, the rational reasons can come and go, but the customer's emotional bond to the brand stays. That's the bond you want to create with your brand personality. You want a brand relationship so emotionally grounded, that no matter how much conflicting information is out there and how many claims are made by your competitors, your customers can honestly defend their choice by saying, "I don't know, I just like it better." How unscientific. How irrational. How human.

Creating an Idealized, Unrealistic Personality

An idealized and unrealistic kind of personality usually emerges from off-site brainstorming meetings in which various personality traits are bandied about and then all the best ones are handwritten on a flip chart. All of this idealization often creates a brand personality that sounds too good to be true. The result can have all the believability of a personal ad in the local newspaper: "Committed, responsible corporation with highly intelligent employees and management seeks long-term relationship with discriminating, insightful, committed customers who want to share a life. We have the aggressiveness of Ted Turner, the foresight of Alan Greenspan, the compassion of the Dalai Lama, the inventiveness of Thomas Edison, and the humility of Mother Teresa." After the participants pat themselves on the back about how great their company is, they disappear for another year until the next off-site meeting.

Unfortunately, during that year, nothing changes. Nothing changes, because the personality is unrealistic and the challenge to execute against that personality is too daunting. For example, if you're as aggressive as Ted Turner, that's fine. Then the other traits that would go along with this kind of personality in real life would probably be a confrontational attitude, street smarts, and innovativeness. Humility, as in the humility of Mother Teresa, would probably not even be on the list.

To add another dimension to the Ted Turner example, one way to make sure your brand personality is believable is to use a real person as a template. Since you're looking for consistency, the use of a real person tends to create a pool of personality traits that go together naturally. A good place to start is to look at the personality of the top one or two people in your company, especially if these people are part of the founding group of entrepreneurs. Generally, the company reflects the personality of one of these people. Dell Computer reflects the personality of Michael Dell; Apple reflects the personality of Steve Jobs. You couldn't use the brand personality of Dell to sell Apple computers, or vice versa. People would know that something was wrong, and the brand would suffer.

If you don't have a clear personality at the top, then look at the people who are respected and rewarded within your company to figure out what traits are valued. If you're a company that rewards people who are incredibly organized—like research firms, accounting firms, and film production companies—then good organizational skill is probably one of your personality traits. A company that thrives on innovation probably rewards its most innovative people with the highest bonuses and the most recognition from management. Look at the other personality traits of these innovative people; words like *focused* or *creative* or *insightful* or *empathetic* will probably come to mind. If you use these words in a description of your brand personality, make sure they represent the whole company and not just one or two extraordinary people.

Tapping into cultural icons is another way to create a brand personality. For example, the cowboy is one of the most potent shorthand cultural symbols in the United States. Marlboro has a brand personality using just a picture of a cowboy and two words: Marlboro Country. We used the cowboy personality for Stuart Anderson's Black Angus restaurants. It was appropriate because the Black Angus logo included an image of a cowboy; cowboy pictures decorated the walls of the restaurants; and the founder, Stuart Anderson, was a rancher.

The personality of the successful immigrant is another part of American cultural mythology. For the Kia Motors America account, we tapped into that mythology. Since Kia was a Korean car company and literally an "immigrant" brand, we used a compilation of the various personality traits of the immigrants who successfully assimilated into American culture. We called the traits the five H's. The traits were humility, hard work, honesty, humanity, and a sense of humor. It turned out that the personality traits of a successful neighborhood Korean grocery store owner were extremely effective in creating a brand personality for a large car company like Kia.

If no single person or cultural icon comes to mind, then the job is a little tougher. Your goal is to have four or five traits that go together naturally. Use your own relationships as a guide. Imagine a friend of yours having the four or five traits you've listed. Does the combination of traits ring true? Do the traits accurately reflect the personality of a real person? If they don't, it's worth spending the time to make sure they do.

Creating Traits That Are Hard to Apply to Marketing Materials

The personality traits that you're looking for have a very practical purpose. They'll be used by a variety of people who will use your specific traits as guides for executing marketing materials, products, events, speeches, Web sites, and various other branding opportunities. Therefore, you'll want to use words that clearly communicate a specific tone and attitude. Using words that you would use to describe a person giving a speech usually works pretty well. For example, "She was dynamic, thoughtful, organized, and funny" are descriptive personality traits that are very helpful when you are creating marketing materials. If you use those kinds of descriptive words when you create your brand personality, you'll be communicating clearly. You'll also have a set of words that make it easier to judge the appropriateness of the tone and attitude of your marketing materials. Instead of saying, "I don't know; I just don't like it," you could say, "This commercial needs to be funnier" or "This speech is too bland; can we make it more confrontational?" or "The music for our sales event is putting me to sleep; can we make it more dynamic?" These are words that designers, copywriters, speech writers, event planners, Web site designers, and ad agencies can understand and utilize when creating your materials.

Creating a Personality That's Outrageous or Provocative without Having the Substance to Back It Up

In the interest of cutting through the clutter or contemporizing their brand, a lot of companies go off the deep end and do something outrageous just for the sake of being outrageous. After years of being told that their brand is too boring, too safe, or too "middle America," these companies go out and hire some hotshot marketing director, design firm, ad agency, or public relations firm and explain, "I want to get noticed." Or they go to an event planner and say, "I want everyone who walks into the convention center to know that we're a hip, hot, talked-about company." Or, looking to attract high-risk investors, they create an annual report that's "leading edge." They do all this without ever changing anything about their company, service, or product. Unfortunately, if your personality is stronger or more provocative than your company really is, then it won't work. This was particularly evident in the dot-com era. In the interest of creating awareness, many times for the sake of attracting investors and not customers, companies created outrageous commercials and events that created name awareness, but never made their name stand for anything other than being outrageous.

If you do have a product or service that's provocative or outrageous, however, then go for it. The use of an outrageous or provocative personality has been very successful for brands like Calvin Klein, Versace, and the Fox Network. Just make sure you have the values, message, and product to back it up.

POOF! YOU'RE A PERSON, NOT A COMPANY

There's one more mind-set you'll need to follow when listing brand personality traits: Think of your company as a person. The reasons that it pays to use this perspective are discussed in the following paragraphs.

People Have an Intuitive Feeling for How Humans Are Supposed to Talk to Other Humans

Although people know how to talk to one another, they don't have that intuition for companies. When most companies communicate in their marketing materials, they tend to talk in corporate-speak, a personality that is decidedly different from the way they talk to people in their day-to-day relationships. Making your company into a person helps you use your innate talents and intuition to avoid that tendency and create a personality that connects with people. That expertise lives in your heart, not your head. Fortunately, that's where the best brands live—in the heart.

Companies Are Like Crowds

Companies are like crowds in that any interaction between them and the customer is often impersonal. When a crowd wants to talk to one person—a referee, quarterback, or singer onstage—the crowd usually yells. Similarly, when one person wants to talk to a crowd, he or she also feels compelled to yell. Yelling seems to be the dynamic in marketing nowadays. When companies want to be heard, they yell. When customers want to be heard, they yell. Turning your company from a crowd into a person will give you a pretty good basis for talking to your audiences without having to resort to yelling.

Companies' and People's Survival Instincts Differ

A company's first instinct for survival is to be profitable. A person's first instinct for survival is to connect with other people. It's important to understand this concept of survival, because under stress—real or imagined—a company will act fundamentally different from a person. You see it all the time when the end of the fiscal quarter comes around and a company doubts that it's going to hit its "numbers." A general panic sets in, core values tend to go out the window, long-term relationships get milked for short-term profits, and the personality of the company turns more aggressive, opportunistic, and desperate than a high school student looking for a date on the morning of the prom. As a result, customers get assailed with e-mails, direct mail, brochures, coupons, and other offers. Suppliers are threatened with a loss of business if they don't drop their margins. The "numbers" suddenly become more important than the relationships. The company does whatever it can to be profitable and survive another quarter, because that's what companies do.

People generally do not act like companies, however. Under stress, people tend to look to connect with other people. That's why towns, cities, and countries were originally formed, so that people could survive the elements and protect themselves against enemies, both real and perceived. For a brand to survive in the marketing jungle, it also needs to resort to the same survival mentality that people have. Its primary source of survival needs to be the survival of the brand relationship. Without that relationship, the brand is vulnerable to "enemies." When your brand gets into a stressful situation, which all brands do from time to time, this survival mind-set provides you with an opportunity to strengthen your relationships with your employees, customers, and investors. It's a great way to create your own brand community.

HOW TO CHOOSE THE RIGHT BRAND PERSONALITY

Before listing the possible brand traits that will make up your brand personality, you should have a copy of your core values and core brand message handy. By referring to them during this exercise, you'll avoid listing personality traits that sound great in isolation, but that are ineffective when it comes to communicating your company's particular values and message. The problem is that you may list personality traits that you personally admire, but that don't accurately reflect your company's true personality. This often happens when a new marketing director, advertising agency, public relations firm, or CEO is hired. Even though nothing has fundamentally changed in the product or service, the brand personality has suddenly changed. The change usually confuses the people who have come to rely on the consistency of that brand's personality in the marketplace and in the workplace. It directly affects the relationship.

POTENTIAL BRAND PERSONALITY TRAITS

The next step is to look at some specific personality traits that might represent your company. Write down about seven or eight traits that feel right, and then we'll narrow that list down to four or five.

In *Building Strong Brands,* David Aaker talks about a brand personality containing such characteristics as gender (Virginia Slims: female, Marlboro: male), age (Apple: young, IBM: older), socioeconomic class (After Eight mints: upscale, Butterfingers: blue-collar), and other classic human traits such as warmth, concern, and sentimentality.[3]

To Aaker's list, I would add the trait of regionality. Many times, the thought of certain regions will make the customer conjure up a whole set of cultural and personality traits. Southern women, Texas ranchers, French perfume, California wine, and Italian furniture all fall into that camp. Knowing the cliché ahead of time will help you determine whether you want to play into the stereotype or counter it.

The following four questions should help you narrow down the possibilities available for your brand and help you choose the traits that are relevant for your brand. After answering these questions, we'll explore the traits that fall into the camp of what Aaker calls the classic human traits.

1. Is your brand male, female, or neither?
2. Is your brand young, middle-aged, old, or for all ages?
3. Is your brand upscale or blue-collar?
4. Is your brand local, regional, national, or global?

The traits listed below are an incomplete list at best, but they cover a range of personality traits instead of digging deeper into the subtleties of each trait. For example, if you choose "warm" or "friendly," when you get down to applying the term to your brand, you'll describe how warm or friendly your brand is. Are you "affectionate" warm—like a new mom with her newborn—or "neighborly" warm—like a Saturn salesperson? Those subtleties are extremely important, but let's deal with the more general traits first.

- ❏ Confident
- ❏ Passionate
- ❏ Warm
- ❏ Friendly
- ❏ Demanding
- ❏ Aggressive
- ❏ Competitive
- ❏ Compassionate
- ❏ Witty
- ❏ Honest
- ❏ Reliable
- ❏ Hardworking
- ❏ Empathetic
- ❏ Creative
- ❏ Trustworthy
- ❏ Dynamic
- ❏ Humble
- ❏ Intelligent

❏ Pragmatic

❏ Idealistic

❏ Emotional

❏ Rational

❏ Community oriented

❏ Tenacious

❏ Optimistic

❏ Direct

❏ Insightful

❏ Street-smart

❏ Thoughtful

❏ Funny

❏ Level-headed

❏ Demanding

❏ Nurturing

❏ Provocative

❏ Skeptical

❏ Opinionated

❏ Loud

❏ Quiet-spoken

❏ Confrontational

An issue that frequently comes up when a company is listing personality traits is what I call the bland-versus-brand personality issue. This situation arises when a company tries to create a personality that doesn't offend anyone, such as when a trait could be misunderstood or perceived as negative. For example, the response to a word like *confrontational* can go like this: "Confrontational? Isn't that a bit strong? People don't like people who are confrontational. Can we change it to collaborative?" It all depends. Some very well liked, well respected brands are built on confrontation. Ralph Nader, Greenpeace, and Mike Wallace of *Sixty Minutes* have all built brands based on confrontation. In the end, you'll want a list of traits that not only engage people, but that inspire commitment. Look for traits that give your personality defined edges. If you're a brand that talks to skateboarders, snowboarders, or surfers, traits like *opinionated, anti-establishment, aggressive,* and *loud* could be appropriate for your brand personality. In that case, there's no need to worry about what the mainstream establishment will think of your personality; they're not your customers. What personality traits can you choose to ensure you have a distinct, clearly defined brand?

CREATING A PERSONALITY THAT CREATES A CONNECTION

In chapter 2, Core Brand Values, you were looking at your internal values. You were looking at three or four values that represented the essence of your company. In this chapter, in addition to looking for the personality traits that define your company, you are also looking for the traits that will communicate those values to others. Therefore, you'll want to include in your set of personality traits at least one trait that has to do with effective communication. Many companies, without considering the importance of communication, will narrow down their personality traits to the four or five that they feel represent them. Unfortunately, many times these traits are not very effective in creating relationships. For example, a company that considers itself a sales company might write down that its personality is "competitive, pragmatic, aggressive, and tenacious." Such a personality might be a great one for achieving short-term sales results, but it might not be the best way to create a long-term relationship with customers or suppliers. Those traits say more about the kind of salespeople the company wants to hire and promote than the kind of relationships it wants to have with its customers. In the absence of any other traits, these traits could very well alienate the very customers who create the repetitive orders that enable a "sales" company to have sales and profits for years to come. In this example, the company might include a personality trait like *empathetic* or *witty* or *personable* or *insightful*. Looking at its salespeople who have created the best customer relationships will help a company determine which traits are most appropriate for its own particular purposes.

Although many companies avoid putting humor in their personality, the use of this trait is one of the fastest ways to be liked. Humor is a positive emotion that enables people to walk away from a piece of communication feeling better than they did before. Humor allows a brand to connect on an emotional level even when it hasn't connected on a rational one. That's one of the reasons so many television commercials use humor. They have thirty seconds to capture a person's attention, get their message across, and be liked in the process. People have become so skeptical of marketing that humor is a way to engage them without getting their guard up. This can be especially true of serious messages. In some cases, serious messages have a better chance of being seen and remembered if they're laced with a smile. The Federal Express campaign that stated, "When it absolutely, positively has to be there overnight" was done in a very slapstick, humorous style, but the message couldn't have been more serious.

Tonight, look at the various television commercials and see how many get your attention through humor. Once they have your attention, notice the message they're communicating. You'll generally find that serious messages like reliability, durability, and product quality are at the heart of the humor. More importantly, notice how you feel about the company that brings you the message. You'll probably find that you like it. After all, what's not to like about a company that's serious about what it does, but doesn't take itself too seriously?

PERSONALIZING YOUR PERSONALITY

Once you've narrowed down your list to four or five personality traits, write a short paragraph after each trait, describing why that personality trait is specifically relevant to your brand. Hopefully the tone and attitude you use in these paragraphs will mirror the personality of your brand and help bring your brand personality to life. Here are some examples from various brand roadmaps that I worked on:

Honest (Kia): "We need to address people's real-world concerns of reliability and durability with real-world testing. In our brochures, we will address people's skittishness about our legitimacy as a car company with 'skeptics boxes.' Whenever possible, we will disarm our audience with honesty. . . . The quickest way to create credibility and believability in the marketplace is to honestly deal with the issues. As they say: 'When all else fails, tell the truth.' "[4]

Direct (Dell Computer): "Our business model is direct and so is our personality. That means we're relentlessly honest, straightforward and 'tell it like it is.' We don't go through middlemen to sell our product, or go through metaphors, analogies or euphemisms to make our point. We state each message simply and directly."[5]

Sense of humor (Stuart Anderson's Black Angus restaurants): "A real cowboy always has a twinkle in his eye. It comes from spending a lot of time outdoors and thinking about things. He knows what's real and what's not. This 'groundedness' lets him see the little quirks and peculiarities in people and comment on them in a humorous way.

"Spending a lot of time alone also means he's got a little trail craziness in him. That's okay. It makes us laugh and keeps him from getting too serious. It also makes him, and our brand, likeable."[6]

Emotional (Beringer Winery): "We should always err on the side of creating an emotional bond. Positive reviews, high ratings and industry awards are wonderful ways of closing the sale, but our first task is to get the consumers to love our brand. As Bill Bernbach [of the original Doyle Dane Bern-bach ad agency] used to say about love, 'the more you analyze it, the faster it disappears.'[7]

"Let's not make that love disappear with too many rational messages. When we talk about getting people to try Beringer wine, let's think in terms of charming, teasing, even seducing the consumer into having a more satisfying, fulfilling experience. More like fine poetry than a detailed wine-making instruction manual. The ability to do that, like the ability to make great wine, is an art. Whenever possible, let's do what we can to inspire and perfect that art."[8]

We're provocative (A Home Away From Homelessness): "We need to make people stop and think about what they don't want to think about: homelessness. We need to make sure every one of our messages is as impactful as it can be. A good rule of thumb is to write an idea down and then sleep on it. If you're not excited about it the next morning, then it's not as impactful as it can be. A bit of risk is encouraged here. It's the only way we're going to cut through the clutter and establish Home Away as true advocates for the homeless in San Francisco."[9]

More high touch than high tech (ShareWave): "When it comes to our personality, we should be parent-friendly. More Dr. Spock than Mr. Spock. We should be the technical experts on home networking, but we should err on the side of being warm, compassionate and understanding of family issues."[10]

These are just a few examples to give you a sense of the length and content of personality statements in your brand roadmap. It's important that you give people a short rationale for why a particular trait is appropriate for your brand. The shorter and clearer the rationale, the more consistent your brand personality will be.

Your Brand Personality

Now that you've looked at various personality traits, write down your thoughts using this worksheet. Once you finish this section, you can more effectively analyze your brand icons.

A. Answer the following questions about your brand.

  1. Is your brand
- ❏ male?
- ❏ female?
- ❏ neither?

  2. Is your brand
- ❏ young?
- ❏ middle-aged?
- ❏ old?
- ❏ for all ages?

3. Is your brand
   - ❏ sophisticated?
   - ❏ mainstream?
   - ❏ down-home?

4. Is your brand
   - ❏ local?
   - ❏ regional?
   - ❏ national?
   - ❏ global?

B. List eight to ten potential brand personality traits.

1.

2.

3.

4.

5.

6.

7.

8.

9.

10.

C. The following questions will help you make sure that you end up with four or five traits that will effectively represent your brand.

1. Do these traits realistically portray your company? (For example, do they represent the traits of the key people in your company? Do they represent the kind of employees who succeed in your company?)

2. Will these traits work across all your marketing materials?

3. Will these traits appeal to your lightning-rod target?

4. Will these traits differentiate you within your category?

5. Do you have at least one personality trait that deals with communication? For example, could you describe someone's speech with the words you've chosen?

D. Now write down the four or five personality traits that you've arrived at for your company. Follow each personality trait with a small paragraph, or notes if you prefer, stating why you believe each trait applies specifically to your company.

1. Personality trait:

2. Personality trait:

3. Personality trait:

4. Personality trait:

5. Personality trait (if necessary):

The next chapter, chapter 5, will help you determine your brand icons.

FIVE

Brand Icons

The identification and clarification of your current brand icons, and possible development of some new ones, will be the last step before you create the actual brand road-map. In this chapter we'll look at the various icons that could represent your particular brand. Although the literal definition of the word *icon* relates to the visual sense, I'm using it in a much broader sense. For the purpose of this exercise, think of a brand icon as anything that is unique to your brand and that brings up an image of your brand in the customer's mind. This image can be triggered by any number of senses, not just sight. For example, smell might be an icon that brings up the brand Starbucks. Touch might be the icon that brings up the brand Velcro. Sound might be the icon that brings up Kellogg's Rice Krispies. We'll look at all the senses to help you define your icons.

This chapter will be more of a macro view of creating icons rather than a detailed exploration of design, music, art direction, and so forth. So many subtleties come into play when a company is creating logos, brochures, packaging, television commercials, and any other type of marketing materials, that short of taking a crash course in design, you'll probably need to enlist the aid of a design firm or an ad agency to refine your choices.

After you work your way through this chapter, you will end up with a good sense of what will work for your brand and what won't. This chapter will also give you a rational structure to evaluate some very subjective areas. It will help you clearly articulate your ideas or concerns to the person or company that's responsible for executing your marketing materials. So many times, businesspeople get as frustrated dealing with artists as artists do with businesspeople. Having a common language helps. This chapter will help give you that language.

HI, MY NAME IS . . .

What's the first thing you do when you want to create a relationship with someone? You tell the person your name, right? The same holds true with brands. Your company name is how people will remember you and refer to you, so by default, it's one of your brand icons. Whenever your name comes up, a certain image of your company will appear in a person's mind.

For starters, then, you want your name to be distinctive and easy to remember. In the world of marketing, with thousands of names careening around the culture and in people's heads, it's a huge advantage to have a name that stands out and is easy to remember. Coke. Pepsi. Saturn. Yahoo! These names have their very own brain cell that they don't have to share with anyone else. When one of these names is mentioned, the mind goes right to that space and stores whatever new information it gets. It's a very efficient way to communicate.

When your name is not as distinctive, or has to compete for space—Goodrich and Goodyear tires, Dreyer's and Breyer's ice cream—the mind flutters a bit before it stores the information you want stored. You want to avoid mind flutter whenever possible.

Your company name, like any name, can also tell people how formal or informal you are. It indicates how approachable you might be. A name gives an indication of personality traits, so evaluating your name against your brand personality traits is a useful exercise. For example, the name IBM, and especially International Business Machines, is less friendly and human than the name Apple. By understanding the perceptions that a name brings up, you can then use your marketing to counteract those perceptions. IBM has done that very effectively with its television commercials and marketing materials. It uses real-life human situations to get across its humanity—a quality that doesn't innately exist in its name.

How unique and memorable is the name of your company? What images come up when you mention its name? If you said the name to someone at a party and came back five minutes later, would the person be able to repeat the name? What emotional response do you get when you mention the name of your company to a stranger? Al Ries and Jack Trout, in their classic book, *Positioning: A Battle for Your Mind,* really delve into the power of a name: "In this positioning era, the single most important marketing decision you can make is what to name the product."[1] Other than substituting the word *brand* for *product,* I couldn't have said it better. So I won't.

USING THE FIVE SENSES MAKE SENSE

After you create awareness with your name, you'll want to introduce as many senses as you can into the brand experience. A multisensory experience is a way for customers to validate their attraction to your brand, an attraction that will be based on a whole body experience rather than just sight or sound. The idea of using the five senses for branding is well documented in Marc Gobe's *Emotional Branding*. In fact, the whole second section of his book is entitled "Sensorial Experiences: The Uncharted Territory of Branding." Gobe describes the need and the justification for the multisensory approach: "Given the competition among today's corporations, it is my feeling that no business can afford to neglect the five senses. Carefully crafted sensory appeals can create that consumer preference that distinguishes a brand amidst a sea of competing commodities."[2]

A complete sensory experience will not only distinguish you, it will make switching brands harder for someone who has committed to your brand. When brands only live in the head, then sometimes all it takes is a simple rational argument to get a customer or an investor to switch. That switch won't happen as easily when the brand relationship includes taste, touch, sight, sound, and smell.

The following areas will help you determine your brand icons. They're categorized according to the five senses. Note the possible areas that might apply to your brand, and then we'll go into detail about the possible strengths, and sometimes weaknesses, of each one.

- Visual (logos, distinctive product or packaging, corporate or product colors, typefaces, designs and layouts, distinct visual techniques, unique architectural images, and clothing)

- Sound (announcers, music, and mnemonics)

- Touch (overall design and form, texture, temperature, and natural versus machine-made)

- Smell

- Taste

Given the thousands of products and services out there, you could consider a lot more options. The main point, however, is for you to think in terms of becoming a multisensory brand with multisensory brand icons. After reading the following sections, you may come up with some opportunities that you hadn't thought of before.

VISUAL ICONS

Since so many companies already have existing visual icons, let's start to look at icons here, in the visual area.

Logos

A logo is a simplified visual symbol that represents a specific product, service, or company. Sometimes the logo is made up of letters that represent the name or acronym of the company, like KFC, IBM, and ABC. Sometimes it's just a visual image, like the Nike swoosh. Sometimes it's a combination of both, like John Deere and FTD.

Since your logo is a simplified symbol of your company, it's a shorthand way for people to know who's talking to them. It helps people find your product or service among thousands of other products and services. But once someone spots your logo, what does the logo mean to that person? Why should he or she remember it? Why should the person believe whatever your company is saying? That's where meaning comes in, and coincidentally, branding. A logo only has meaning if your company has meaning to that person. As a visual image in the brain, the logo becomes a magnet for personal experiences with the brand. The logo can trigger memories, opinions, rumors, or personal experiences with a brand. Consequently, as you're moving through this chapter, it's important that you understand what your logo is communicating, both as a symbol in isolation—for new customers—and as a consistent image of your brand for existing customers. Only then can you know whether your logo is an asset, a neutral influence, or a liability to your brand. Only then can you know whether your logo is helping you communicate what you want to communicate.

What do I mean by "helping you communicate what you want to communicate"? Let's say you've determined that innovation is a key part of your core message. It's the driving principle behind your company and a key trait that you look for in new employees. But upon examining your logo, you conclude that it looks boring, dated, or unimaginative. Then your logo might be a liability as you move forward, because it's not communicating what you want it to communicate. In fact, it counteracts your core message and becomes a visual reminder of how "not innovative" you are. This is especially problematic with potential customers who don't know your company. It can also be a problem whenever your logo is seen in isolation, without the added information of a television commercial, a brochure, or an annual report that might highlight your company's innovations. In this case, you have some options:

- You could update or redesign your logo.

- You could downplay the size of your logo in your marketing materials and demonstrate your innovation with your packaging, your layouts, or even your choices of colors.

- You could create a slogan that goes with your logo and highlights your core message of innovation.

The point isn't whether your logo is good or bad, but merely whether it's helping you achieve your brand objectives. There are a number of ways to compensate for any weakness of your logo, but you need to be aware of the strengths and weaknesses in relation to your overall brand direction.

Distinctive Product or Packaging

The overall look, shape, size, or type of materials can also bring up an image of your brand: Consider the unique look of the Apple Cube, the Wham-O Frisbee, L'eggs stockings, and Hershey's Kisses. In the car category, distinctive designs are constantly used to force people to reevaluate their perception of a particular brand. The Dodge Viper, the Volkswagen Beetle, and Chrysler's Prowler come to mind. Distinctive products can communicate a brand personality, a set of values, and in many ways, a brand message louder than any ad or television commercial ever could. Do you have any products or packaging that you can leverage for your brand? Does your brand lend itself to a unique product or package that could represent the values of your brand? What impact could you make in your marketplace with a new look in your packaging, or a little more innovation in the design of your products?

Corporate or Product Colors

Colors instantly communicate certain messages about your brand. Because of this instinctual response, it's important to determine whether your colors are helping or hurting the effectiveness of the messages you want to communicate about your brand. We'll begin by looking at colors from a macro point of view. Once you're in the ballpark of a certain area of color, you'll probably want to hire a color consultant or designer to fine-tune your color choices. Some questions you'll want to address involve the level of sophistication of the colors, their distinctiveness within their category, and whether the colors elicit the right emotional response.

Are the Colors Simple or Sophisticated? Simple colors are the primary and secondary colors on the color wheel (red, yellow, blue, orange, green, and purple). Sophisticated colors are all the other colors (taupe, mauve, sea green, slate blue, maroon, pumpkin, sage, etc.).

Simple colors tend to be more vibrant and shout louder than do sophisticated colors. Think of the original Crayola box with only eight colors. Jamba Juice uses simple colors. Toys"R"Us uses simple colors. Traffic signs around the world use really simple colors to stand out along the highway—red, blue, green, caution yellow, and orange.

For sophisticated colors, think of the Crayola box with sixty-four colors. Brands like Laura Ashley, Armani, Tiffany, and Jaguar use sophisticated colors. The colors quickly communicate a certain understated elegance and, in many ways, set up the expectation of a quieter, more intimate conversation. The rich colors of Starbucks shops create a much different coffee experience from that represented by the simple colors of McDonald's.

Knowing your brand personality can help here. If your personality is aggressive, loud, or dynamic, then simple colors can help reinforce those qualities. If your brand personality is a little more reserved and thoughtful, then sophisticated colors will reinforce those qualities.

Are the Colors Differentiating Within Your Category? As you exit the freeway and look for a gas station, notice how the colors help you find the different brands (figure 5-1). There's the red, white, and blue

FIGURE 5 - 1

Visual Branding

There are a lot of visual ways to stand out. Imagine the marked box in bright red. Creating a different value from that of the environment around your message is another way to stand out. For example, newspapers usually have an overall value of medium gray because of all the small type. To stand out, use big black type (as newspapers do when they have big news), or create white space that isolates your message and draws attention to it.

Draw attention to your brand

Chevron sign on one corner; the green and yellow British Petroleum sign on another; the yellow and red Shell sign on another; and the orange and blue Union 76 sign on yet another. The same visual differentiation holds true when you are trying to spot your rental car company at the airport: Hertz, Avis, National, and Budget all have colors that you can spot a block away.

Supermarkets are excellent classrooms for color differentiation. Stand at the end of an aisle, and see if you can spot the Clorox bleach bottle. From the end of the cereal aisle, can you tell if the store carries Wheaties, Corn Pops, Frosted Flakes? Can you see if the store carries Campbell's soup if you are standing at the end of another aisle? This brand differentiation is all done with simple, distinctive blocks of color.

Are your company's colors as differentiating in your category as the colors chosen by oil companies, car rental companies, and package-goods companies? If they aren't, you've missed an opportunity to stand out from the crowd.

Are the Colors Eliciting the Right Emotional Response? The topic of brand psychology is too big to cover in depth in this book, but it's important to realize that the colors you choose are creating an emotional response in your audience. In an excellent book, *A Natural History of the Senses,* Diane Ackerman talks about how scientists have known for years how certain colors trigger an emotional response in people. She mentions everything from the use of "passive pink" in hospitals and schools, to "greenrooms" that have a restful effect on talk-show guests, to people's having a grip that's 13.5 percent stronger than normal when looking at a red light in a testing situation.[3] Marc Gobe's *Emotional Branding* also addresses the specific emotions that various brands have tapped into with their brand colors. Knowing what emotion you would like your customers to feel is a great way to determine the appropriateness of the colors you choose. It will also help you communicate with the color consultants, designers, and other experts who are responsible for clearly communicating the feeling and message you want to communicate.

Typefaces

The choice of which typefaces to use to communicate the essence of a company is one area that tends to get overlooked because most businesspeople don't have the vocabulary to articulate their needs. Typeface decisions usually get relegated to a design firm, an ad agency, or a Web site designer. But since the typeface is a critical element in developing a brand, you need to have a general sense of what's being communicated with your typeface and make sure it's reinforcing your brand personality. For a more complete explanation of the world of type, I recommend Kit Hinrichs's *Typewise*, an extremely visual and easy-to-understand book about type.[4]

At the risk of being overly simplistic, we can divide typefaces into two basic groups: serif and sans serif (figure 5-2). The typeface you're reading right now is serif type. Serifs are the little feet that the type sits on and that cap off a letter. Those little feet help your eye move from letter to letter. Because of that movement, serif type is easier to read when you have lots of type to read. You'll find that newspapers, books, and most magazines almost exclusively use serif type when they tell their stories.

Sans serif type is type without serifs. The "United We Brand" type on the cover of this book is sans serif type. As Hinrichs explains, sans serif type was invented when modern furniture and modern buildings were designed: "Sans-serif type became prominent during

FIGURE 5-2

Which Type Is Your Type?

Serif typefaces tend to have more curves and little feet (serifs) that help move your eye from one letter to the next. Because of the more organic feel of the letter and the ease of moving from one letter to the next, the typeface tends to be viewed as friendlier.

 Sans serif typefaces are like modern furniture. The adornments have been stripped away, and the letter has been simplified down to its essence. Because of the lack of adornments and because of the self-contained character of each letter, sans serif type is customarily viewed as less friendly.

serif
sans serif

the twentieth century's Machine Age. Its streamlined, hard-edged look implied efficiency and serifs were viewed as superfluous and unnecessary."[5] Because the letter is stripped down to its essence, each letter is an individual that doesn't really lead your eye to the next letter. Your eye has to hop from letter to letter, so the type is slightly harder to read. Sans serif type is generally used for shorter messages like titles, headlines, or other text that tends to be a paragraph or less in length. Sans serif type is also good for situations in which the type is seen at a distance, because the details—in this case the serifs—tend to disappear anyway. That's why sans serif letters are used on highway signs. That's also why sans serif type gets used quite a bit in Web site designs, especially with smaller type. With the low resolution of the computer screens, serifs tend to get lost.

 Because of these innate differences in style, serif and sans serif typefaces communicate a visceral sense of either being personal or impersonal. Serif typefaces tend to be more personal, in the same way that a piece of furniture that has some curves, eccentricities, and adornments feels more personal. Sans serif typefaces tend to be more impersonal, in the same way that a modern office chair made of tubular chrome and black leather seems more impersonal. Both styles can be well designed, beautiful, and useful, but they send very different emotional messages.

Because of the readability differences between serif and sans serif type, you'll want to decide how much text you may need to communicate your various messages—from your ads to your Web site to your annual report to your brochures—when considering typefaces. If you anticipate that you'll need longer copy in some of your marketing materials, then you should probably have at least one serif typeface in your brand toolbox. Too many companies make brand typeface decisions based on letterheads, business cards, and signage—pieces that have very little type—and then find out that those typefaces don't work very well when a longer story needs to be told. So before you settle on a specific type, have a couple of pages set in eleven-point type and see how easy or hard the material is to read.

If you decide to make a truly unique branding statement with your typeface, you should enlist the aid of a professional designer. So many options come into play, that you'll want to make sure that the typeface has enough weights, sizes, and variations to give you the flexibility you'll need for different media, different documents, and different headings within those documents. For example, some typefaces have no italics version, so quotes and captions would have to be handled differently. Since not all typefaces come in different weights (extra bold, bold, semibold, medium, light, and extra light), you would need to figure out other ways to call attention to subheads and captions you might want to make bold. To protect yourself, ask to see all the different weights and styles of that particular typeface. It's better to have too many choices within a typeface rather than too few. Better yet, go to an expert with your brand values, message, and personality to see what solutions they bring to the table.

Design and Layout

Design and layout are areas that are powerful branding icons. A good exercise is to get all your marketing materials and pin them up on the wall. Then sit back, look at the whole wall, and get an overall impression. Is there cohesiveness among all the various materials? Do certain colors pop out? Do certain design elements repeat themselves? Is the overall design fairly rigid and gridlike or more fluid and loose? Are the designs more visually oriented or text oriented? Do you tend to feature products or people?

These types of questions will tell you which parts of your design and layouts could be brand icons. Now look at your core values, core message, and brand personality. Which design elements reinforce those brand objectives, and which ones don't? For example, if you've defined your company as people oriented, but your layouts are so rigid and gridlike that it looks as if a robot designed them, then you might want to loosen up your layouts. If you're a people-oriented company but you only show your products, then you might want to look for ways to add some human touches to your layouts.

Once you've done this exercise with your own materials, do the same thing with the marketing materials from your competition. Advertising agencies and design firms routinely look at the competition's materials when working on a new account. It gives them a snapshot of the category and helps them see the visual opportunities that will make their brand stand out. Including your own materials with the competition's is also an eye-opening experience. If you're a university that wants your admissions materials to stand out, lay out all the admissions packets of your competition, and you'll immediately see what students, parents, and high-school counselors see. This exercise helped The Branson School create a very distinctive admissions packet compared with those of other private high schools in the San Francisco area.

Distinctive layouts can be as powerful as distinctive packaging. Absolut Vodka understands this and has kept the same format for more than twenty years. *National Geographic* has kept the distinctive yellow border on its magazine for more than ninety years. Try the comparison exercise with your own marketing materials. It's a great way to find your visual niche in the marketplace.

Distinct Visual Techniques

A distinct visual technique is a quick way to stand out in a cluttered environment. IBM puts a blue band at the top and bottom of its television commercials and shoots its film in black and white. If you walked across the room, turned off the sound, stood on your head, and looked at the commercial, you'd still know it was an IBM commercial. That's a distinct visual technique. J. Peterman Company used loose illustrations instead of photographs in its catalog to capture the look and feel of its clothing. This technique was unique and distinctive within the fashion industry.

Magazines are very good at using this technique to stand out. *The New Yorker* has a distinctive brand image because of the whimsical, illustrative nature of its covers. *Cosmopolitan* has a very different look because of the simple, sexy photographic style it uses. *Wired* magazine uses fluorescent inks to recreate the electric buzz of the digital age.

Creating a distinct visual technique can help you make sure that the brand image you project in the marketplace is distinctly yours. When that look comes directly out of your brand personality, as it does with *The New Yorker, Cosmopolitan,* and *Wired,* then it's even more powerful.

Unique Architectural Images

Architecture can be a brand icon. The Transamerica Building has its pyramid shape. The Guggenheim Museum in New York has its Frank Lloyd Wright–designed spiral ramp. In fact, more and more museums are mirroring their core value of showcasing creativity and are becoming works of art themselves. The Guggenheim Museum Bilbao, San Francisco Museum of Modern Art, and Museum of Contemporary Art, Los Angeles, are current examples.

Universities can also become synonymous with distinctive buildings, monuments, and stadiums. The University of California at Berkeley has its Campanile. Yale has *The Women's Table,* designed by Maya Lin.

Small businesses, like Doggie Diner, use distinctive signage to separate themselves from their competitors. Large corporations use larger expressions of their brand, like the United Airlines Terminal at Chicago's O'Hare International Airport, to communicate their uniqueness. Cities have branded themselves with architecture for centuries. The Parthenon, the Eiffel Tower, and Big Ben all instantly communicate the uniqueness of Athens, Paris, and London.

Companies can tap into their architecture in the same way. Architecture tends to communicate certain core values much more believably than just a logo does. There's something about concrete, stone, and metal that really communicates stability and commitment more believably than just ink on paper does. Study your own architecture and your brand objectives, and see if a brand icon appears.

Clothing

Clothing says a lot about a brand. For years, IBM was associated with white shirts and ties. Dell, during its first few years of business, wanted to be taken seriously and demanded that its workers wear white shirts and ties, just like the IBM employees. Apple, on the other hand, had engineers walking around in worn-out jeans and T-shirts. People could get a sense of each brand just by walking through the building. The clothing said a lot about core values, the core message, and the brand personality of each company.

Many organizations, from sports teams to religious groups to rock groups to restaurants, use clothing as brand icons. It can be a powerful differentiator in the marketplace. Walk onto a Southwest Airlines plane, and what do you see? Comfortable, colorful clothing that communicates the feeling of the Southwest. The clothing communicates as much about Southwest's brand, and its respect for its employees, as its logo does.

If you think that clothing could be a branding tool for your company, go back to thinking about your company as a person. How would you dress that person? Not necessarily specifically, but in more macro terms, like business dress or casual? Natural materials or synthetic? One specific color or a corporate palette? Rigid rules or individual interpretation? These more general areas should help you narrow your focus and effectively communicate the values and personality you want to communicate.

SOUND ICONS

Announcer (Also Known as a Voice-Over)

The voice of your brand carries the tone and attitude of whatever your company is saying. From that voice, people will get a sense of where you're from, what you believe, and whether they want to listen to you. Your brand voice should be a direct translation of your brand personality.

In spite of the importance of voice, many companies short-change themselves when it comes to choosing a voice that will communicate their various messages. At our ad agency, we would literally go through hundreds of voices to find one voice that would uniquely represent a particular client in the marketplace.

In many ways, the same questions you used to create your brand personality are the same questions you'll use to determine the voice of your brand. For example, is the voice of your company male or female? Is the voice of your company young, middle-aged, or old? Is the voice local, regional, national, or international? Is it sophisticated or down-home, soothing or edgy? Is your voice distinctive, or does it remind you of another brand? There are no absolute right or wrong answers, only right or wrong choices for your brand. There are as many different voices as there are people, but most companies keep going to the same voice-over talent that everyone else uses. Because of this conformity, every brand starts sounding like every other brand.

A good test is to listen to a voice without any visual distractions. Motel 6 has been very successful at creating a unique voice for its brand with Tom Bodett because the motel chain established its brand voice through the radio. If you need to choose a voice to represent your brand, get a cassette and listen to it in your car. It's a very effective way to get an overall impression of the credibility and likability of a voice you might be considering.

Once you settle on a voice, use it across as many media platforms and branding opportunities as possible—television commercials, sales videos, sales training tapes, radio, interactive displays—and if possible, put it on your company's voice mail or answering machine. Ultimately, your brand voice should be so distinctive that your customers can recognize your brand without ever seeing the brand logo. If your brand voice can pass that test, then you have a voice that could become a very powerful brand icon for you.

Music

If you want to get people hooked on a feeling, use music. Music creates an emotional context for whatever you're saying. The movie industry uses music very effectively. When directors want to scare you, they play spooky, scary music. If they want you to feel sad, they play sad, lonely music. If they want you to get swept away with the action, they'll play a full orchestral score to sweep you away in sound. Close your eyes at the beginning of a comedy, and you'll be able to tell instantly that it's a comedy. Music is one of the quickest ways to communicate the emotion you want people to feel. That's an important marketing tool because you generally don't have a lot of time to create an emotional connection. In television, for example, you have anywhere from ten to sixty seconds to create a positive emotional response. Music can help. While the mind is paying attention to the announcer delivering the rational message and the eyes are occupied by the visuals, music can sit in the background and direct a person's feelings. It can viscerally communicate nostalgia, humor, sadness, hopefulness, and patriotism, to name a few. As a tool for branding products or companies, music has been terribly underutilized.

Broadcast companies understand the power of music. Every new radio or television show has a theme song. When you end up liking the show, whenever the theme song comes on, it's like curling up in a warm blanket on a cold night. It's familiar, comforting. You look forward to spending the next half hour or hour with that brand.

What's your company's theme song? Can you hum it (the sign of a good melody)? If you have a business or retail establishment, does the music help create a distinctive environment? In *Emotional Branding,* Marc Gobe talks about the power of music to create a brand by creating an environment, especially among Generation X and Generation Y shoppers. For example, Canal Jean Co. in Manhattan hires live DJs to give the store a clublike feeling. Gobe also describes how Abercrombie & Fitch uses fast and lively music to create a youthful environment.[6]

If you need help, go to an arranger or a musician who creates music for a living. Having a clear idea of your brand personality, and particularly the emotional response you want to get from your audience, will help you end up with a piece of music that captures the feeling of your brand. There are also companies now specializing in creative music programs that enhance a brand's specific image. AEI Music Network uses its library of more than seven million songs to help you create a customized music environment.[7]

Mnemonics

Besides voice-overs and music, mnemonics is another way to capture the sound of your brand. A mnemonic is a short rhyme, phrase, musical clip, or other technique for reinforcing your brand message. Sometimes it's the sound of the product itself, like the rev of a Porsche engine at the end of a television commercial. Sometimes it's a sound effect that reinforces a brand message. For example, in some of Ford's television commercials, the voice-over "Ford trucks are built Ford tough" is followed by the sound of a power drill tightening the nuts on the four bolts holding the Ford logo. A mnemonic could also be a phrase that's repeated over and over until it becomes associated with the brand. What brand pops into your mind when you hear, "Snap! Crackle! Pop!"?

If you can create a simple mnemonic that helps people remember you, it's a great tool to use. Sprint has used the "sound of a pin dropping" for years. Whenever we see and hear it, that mnemonic reminds us of Sprint's brand message: clear, nonstatic digital reception. For Sprint, it's like running a little minicommercial at the end of its regular commercial.

The music industry understands this technique and uses it all the time. They call it a musical *hook*. It's a simple lyric or melody that embeds itself in a person's mind and takes on a life of its own. When you hear that hook, you start singing or humming the whole song, sometimes whether you want to or not. The same holds true with brand mnemonics.

What's your "hook"? Does your brand have a distinct product noise that you could use? Is there a sound effect that could capture the essence of your core message? Is there a simple melody line that you could use at the end of your video and audio materials that could become a brand icon? The use of sound is a very sound way to create a brand.

TOUCH ICONS

The sense of touch is another sensory aspect often ignored in communicating a brand message. A product's form, its texture, the temperature associated with a product or service (e.g., the heat provided by a gas company and the cold provided by a beer), and other senses of touch offer powerful possibilities for communicating a message.

Overall Design and Form

Some products just feel better. Shave with a Braun shaver, and the razor just feels better in your hand. Wear a cashmere Armani sport coat, and it fits and feels better. I remember the first time I sat in the leather bucket seat of my dad's Volvo 1800 after learning to drive in the L-shaped, vinyl seats of our family's American-made station wagon. I felt secure. The seat formed around me, and I felt safer. Feeling safer is a good experience for a brand that has safety as its core brand value. "Touch" made me feel that safety.

Does your brand have a certain design that people can really feel? Are some of your product attributes more experiential than rational? Is there a way you can translate that touch into your marketing materials?

When our advertising agency—Chiat/Day San Francisco—was given the assignment of introducing the Reebok Pump, we knew that the shoes felt different from any other athletic shoe. When the sneakers were pumped up, people said the shoes seemed to fit better and give more support. Consequently, all we had to do with the ads and commercials was create incredible awareness so that people would look for the shoes in the store and feel the actual shoe for themselves. Anything we would have said to try to convince someone that the shoe fit better or gave better support would have paled in comparison to how the shoe felt on the person's foot, so we didn't try. We just said, "It fits a little better than your ordinary athletic shoe," and created incredible awareness—and controversy—with our introductory television commercial.

If your brand has a certain design or shape that "feels" different, use the sense of touch to your advantage. The personal, interactive nature of someone touching your product creates an emotional and physical connection that is hard to duplicate or compete against. That makes touch a very powerful brand icon.

Texture

You might not consider texture an obvious brand icon, but it can be a key differentiator for your brand. Does your brand have a texture?

To introduce the Reebok Pump, we created a commercial called the "Reebok Bungee" spot. I was the art director and creative director of the spot, and Jeff Billig was the writer. Although the commercial only ran six times, it sold out every Reebok Pump in the nation (at $180 a pair) and shoe production was doubled. If you didn't see the commercial, the premise was simple. We had two guys jump off a bridge with bungee cords attached to their ankles. One guy wore Nikes, and the other guy wore the new Reebok Pumps. The cameras followed their flight down. When they got to the bottom, there was only one guy left, swinging back and forth as the announcer says, "The Reebok Pump. It fits a little better than your ordinary athletic shoe." The spot created quite a stir. Ironically, the networks pulled the spot off the air because of complaints, yet they kept showing it for free on their news programs. The commercial also created incredible awareness for the product. Arsenio Hall, host of the popular *Arsenio Hall Show,* did a twelve-minute segment on the commercial the day after it ran. National magazines and newspapers carried articles about the commercial. This was in 1990, before bungee jumping was even known in most circles and before extreme sports became such popular fare on regular TV. Paul Fireman, CEO of Reebok, estimated that the spot generated more than $30 million in free publicity and media exposure. The commercial cost only $500,000 in actual media dollars. Not a bad return on investment. All this fuss was from a commercial created just so that people could go in and experience the shoes for themselves.

Is texture unique to your brand, as it is for a brand like Jell-O? In addition to design and form, communicating the texture of your brand can make people want to touch and feel your product. Notice the difference between the texture of Quaker oatmeal and Nabisco Cream of Wheat? Feel the grit of Lava soap? These textures help define the brands.

Are there any textures that your brand represents? If there are, perhaps some of them can be translated into your marketing materials. For example, if your brand texture is smooth, then perhaps your marketing materials should be smooth. If your company values the natural world—like Eddie Bauer, Patagonia, or the Sierra Club—then perhaps your marketing materials should reflect that naturalness. Using textured, recycled paper could help your brand communicate those core values.

If you're having a hard time determining textures for your company, think of your competitors' textures. Study brands that are similar to yours to see which textures they highlight. Texture is a great way for people to literally get a feel for your product. It also enables you to tap into a direct sensory experience that can create a unique impression for your brand.

Temperature

What temperature is best suited for your product or service? See if you can make it part of your brand experience. Corona beer is sold by juxtaposing the heat of a Mexican beach with the image of a cold bottle of Corona. Patagonia sells winter wear by showing cozy people in freezing environments.

If you have products that are forged in heat, then let the customer feel it. If you have products that are supposed to make a person feel warm and cozy, then create marketing materials that are warm and cozy.

If any of these examples spark some ideas for your brand, take a few minutes to write them down. Then use that list to come up with some more ideas of your own. Tomorrow, revisit the list to see if any ideas stand out as ways to make your brand a little more distinctive in the marketplace.

Natural Versus Machine-Made

Some products feel natural. When they touch your skin, they feel real. Cotton has that feel. Real wood has it. So does soft leather. Reebok built a good part of its brand reputation in the 1980s by introducing soft leather to athletic shoes.

If you make natural or real products, you have an opportunity to let your marketing materials reflect those core values. For example, at guitar shows I've attended, some craftsmen who make handmade guitars have given me slick business cards with a plastic-like feel to them. Every time I hold their cards, my physical reaction counteracts all the naturalness that exists in their products.

However, if you have slick and modern products, then reinforce those qualities in your materials. Car companies mirror the technology of their cars by using high-tech, high-gloss materials when they create their brochures and showroom displays. The Sharper Image also surrounds its high-tech gadgets with an environment that's high-tech and high-gloss.

Given the visceral feeling that people get from touching the materials you use throughout your brand, you should consciously examine your materials to see if they're communicating the values, message, and personality you want to project as a brand. Going through that process will also enable you to clearly communicate the feel you want in all your marketing materials.

SMELL ICONS

It's time to wake up and smell the opportunities. As Diane Ackerman describes in *A Natural History of the Senses,* "Nothing is more memorable than a smell. . . . Smells detonate softly in our memory like poignant landmines, hidden under the weedy mass of many years and experiences. Hit a tripwire of smell, and memories explode all at once."[8] Imagine having that "detonation" be a part of your customer's brand experience. Brands in the perfume category understand this. Flower shop owners understand the attraction and power of fresh-cut flowers. If your product doesn't have a distinctive smell, perhaps you're missing a branding opportunity. Smell can create a sense of environment that defines your brand. Lemon-scented Pledge, for example, isn't just a scent to differentiate itself from other similar products; it's a smell that helps define who that person is when someone visits his or her home. Walk into a Starbucks coffee shop, and the smell will communicate more about the quality of the brand's products than any print ad or mission statement ever could.

People can definitely get a sense of whether a brand is "for them" from the smell. But once they accept the smell as "for them," the continued use of the smell can be a powerful way to create brand loyalty and a long-term customer.

TASTE ICONS

Taste is an obvious brand icon for companies that deal with food and beverages: McDonald's french fries, Oreo cookies, Altoid mints, Celestial Seasonings teas, Ben & Jerry's ice creams, and Jack Daniel's whiskey. Every brand in the food and beverage industry wants to create a specific taste associated with its brand.

The ability of a company to make its taste a specific customer's taste is a very powerful branding device. Once a company's taste gets stored as "my taste" in someone's long-term memory, it's amazing how passionate and adamant that person will become when defending his or her choice. Even in the face of blind taste-test results and scientific evidence to the contrary, people will defend their choice of being a Pepsi or Coke person. In some cases, they would rather have nothing at all than change to some other brand. In the ice cream category, people drive miles out of their way to get Dreyer's Rocky Road ice cream rather than settle for a competitor's version. Taste is apparently so personal and subjective, that once you're in, you're in. That kind of brand loyalty is priceless.

What tastes are associated with your brand? What memories can be brought to the surface with those tastes? How loyal are people to your brand's specific taste?

Although this discussion of the sensory aspects of brand icons is far from complete, it may help you come up with some ideas you hadn't thought of before. Being a multisensory brand is a powerful way to communicate with people on many levels: emotional, sensory, literal, visceral, psychological, environmental, and experiential. It's a way for people to personalize your brand for themselves. Different people rely on different senses to validate their experiences. When people are allowed to use their own sensory strengths to make a decision about a brand, they tend to trust their brand decision-making process to a greater degree. Giving them that option can make for a brand loyal customer.

THE POWER OF CRAVINGS

Cravings can be ignited by any or all of the senses. Sometimes, cravings can come at certain points in the day. Other times, they're triggered by an emotional state of mind or a certain location.

Companies can use brand icons as triggers for the specific craving that applies to their brand. A "cheese pull" (a camera shot of a cheese-laden slice being pulled from a pizza) in a pizza commercial can trigger the craving for a pizza. Hearing the "pffft!" of a beer bottle being opened can trigger a craving for a cold beer. The smell of freshly mown grass can trigger a desire to go see a major league baseball game. As human beings, we all have cravings switches that can be triggered.

To use the power of cravings for communicating your brand, first look at the specific cravings that could be unique to your category or product. For example, certain types of food within the food category are known as craving foods: Mexican food, pizza, ice cream, chocolate, and snack foods fall into that camp. When you're at a ballpark, hot dogs can become a craving. Movie theaters are linked with the smell of popcorn. When you get a craving in those environments, it's hard to shake the desire to indulge.

There are also macro cravings that we have as human beings: the cravings for human connection, for survival, for shelter, for acceptance, and for comfort. You can make use of these basic human cravings when developing your brand icon. If you're marketing in a hot climate, then your air-conditioning could become a brand icon that satisfies the comfort craving. If your customers come from an area where people tend to be isolated, creating a community area in your store or restaurant might be a way for people to satisfy their need to connect with other people. Perhaps your product has sugar or caffeine; it then satisfies the craving for instant energy in the late afternoon. Even a craving *not* to have cravings is a craving. Companies that specialize in diets, retreats, clinics, or exercise can leverage those needs for their brands. More importantly, they can satisfy those cravings for their customers and create a relationship in the process.

Have any cravings shown up in your exploration of the five senses? If so, try to find ways to make them an integral part of your marketing.

THE POWER OF CEOS AND BRAND CHARACTERS

What do Anita Roddick, Richard Simmons, the Energizer Bunny, Paul Newman, Tony the Tiger, the Jolly Green Giant, the Marlboro Man, Betty Crocker, and the MGM Lion have in common? They're all brand icons. These people or characters represent the essence of their brand. They all bring a specific set of values, messages, and personality to their brand. When you see or hear these icons, whatever is said or done is tied to their brand. So if you're going to go down this path, it's important to make sure that the icons truly represent the important qualities of your brand. Tony the Tiger isn't going to hold out for an unseemly amount of money or get in a fight at the local bar or sell his services to the highest bidder. As a brand icon, he's ggggreeeaaaatttt!

CEOs, on the other hand, don't always have the dependability of Tony the Tiger. They can be great brand icons as long as they truly represent the core values of your brand and are going to stick around for a while. In recent years, too many high-profile CEOs, when their company starts to falter, disappear faster than you can say, "Hand me my golden parachute, please." Inevitably, these frequent changes at the helm hurt the brand, which is created through consistency, commitment, and a strict adherence to core brand values.

Even though characters, CEOs, and mascots can be effective brand icons, it's important that you look ahead five to ten years from now to judge whether your brand can be encapsulated in a single person or character. If it can't, then you might want to avoid those brand icons. If your brand can benefit in the long term from these icons, then go for it.

PERSONALIZING YOUR BRAND ICONS

Once you have a set of brand icons, you'll need to divide them into major icons and minor ones. Major icons are the ones you always use. They generally include your company name, logo, packaging, tag line, company colors, voice-over, and typeface. Minor icons are those that you can use opportunistically. For example, taste, touch, and smell are senses that might be utilized wherever a customer has direct contact with your brand. Starbucks utilizes the smell of coffee. KFC allows the smell of fried chicken to waft around the neighborhood. By dividing your list of icons this way, you're clearly communicating to your designers, ad agency, and marketing people which icons are mandatory.

Once you've divided your list into major and minor icons, write a short paragraph after each icon, explaining why that icon is important for your brand. Here are some examples from a variety of brand roadmaps that were created at Goldberg Moser O'Neill:

The food (Stuart Anderson's Black Angus): "We're proud of our food. That's why we feature it so prominently in our commercials and marketing materials. Close-ups are preferred because they say quality. And even though we're proud that we sell all-inclusive meals, we should err on the side of having the steak be the center of attention, with all the other food filling in as the supporting cast. Appetite appeal is everything. If we haven't got the consumer drooling over our photography, we haven't done our job."[9]

Informative layouts (Dell Computer): "Our layouts should always err on the side of directness and clarity. No one has ever been confused into parting with his or her money.

Or their company's money. When all else fails, simplify.
It works."[10]

The human touch (Acoustic Disc—Independent record label):

"The human touch adds personality and warmth. It could be a true human story. It could be a picture of a human being. It could be 'handmade' items rather than computer-generated ones. It can be as simple as adding a little 'imperfection' that gives our materials a feeling that they've been touched by a human being, not just dropped into a grid by a computer.

For example, design elements that break planes, bleed off the page, or are slightly tilted (like our logo) give a sense of those human dynamics. Whenever we can give the impression that we're a small group of passionate artists creating art versus a giant faceless corporation turning out mass-produced pseudo-art, the more likeable we'll be as a brand."[11]

Not all your brand icons need a description, but it helps. For example, if your logo really doesn't have a reason, then don't go into an explanation. Just mention that it's a key icon, and leave it at that.

Your Brand Icons

Before we look at how you're going to take all the pieces you've assembled—brand values, brand message, brand personality, and brand icons—and put them together to create your very own brand roadmap, let's go through the worksheet and get your brand icons down on paper.

A. List your possible brand icons below:

  1. Brand name:

  2. Brand logo:

  3. Distinctive product or packaging:

Worksheet: Your Brand Icons

4. Company colors:

5. Company typefaces:

6. Design and layout:

7. Distinct visual techniques (like the IBM blue bars on its television commercials):

8. Unique architectural images:

9. Clothing:

10. Announcer (also known as a voice-over):

11. Music styles or songs:

12. Mnemonics:

13. Product design that's tactile:

14. Product textures:

15. Product temperatures:

16. Natural or handmade feeling:

17. Unique aromas:

18. Unique tastes:

19. Unique, identifiable CEO, character, or mascot:

B. For each of your major brand icons, write a short paragraph or description of why that particular icon is representative of the values, message, and personality of your brand.

1. Major icon:

2. Major icon:

3. Major icon:

4. Major icon:

5. Major icon:

C. Do the same exercise with your minor brand icons. This exercise gives your designers and marketing people some more options to add depth to your brand.

1. Minor icon:

2. Minor icon:

3. Minor icon:

4. Minor icon:

D. Finally, go over your list one last time, and ask yourself the following questions:

1. Do I have at least one of each of the five senses listed (sight, sound, touch, smell, and taste)?

2. Are there any icons that tap into people's cravings (e.g., a taste or smell)? If there are, you might want to highlight them in some way so that people can focus on this area when the opportunity arises.

The next chapter will help you start putting all the pieces together to create your own brand roadmap.

SIX

Your Brand Roadmap

If you have followed the steps presented in the book up to this point, you are now ready to draw together all your hard work to create a brand roadmap. Your goal will be a practical, day-to-day guide for your brand—a guide that can sit on everyone's desk for easy, frequent use. To accomplish that goal, you'll look at the overall layout of the information. You'll need to make sure that the tone and attitude of the brand roadmap are consistent with your brand personality. You'll look at the importance of adding visuals or other sensory icons. (Too many times, companies try to explain the whole breadth of their brand with only words when other sensory signals can help simplify and humanize the communication.) You'll also decide whether your brand roadmap would benefit from the addition of other elements, such as an FAQ (frequently asked questions) section. By the end of this chapter, your brand roadmap will be well on the path of being a living, breathing example of your brand.

To start the process, put all the critical brand information onto one sheet of paper. Start by listing the three or four core values, then your core message, followed by three to five brand personality traits, and then list your brand icons. At this point, putting all your brand information on one page can help you see the consistencies, inconsistencies, and redundancies that inevitably turn up. Many times, companies repeat a certain trait in their core values and brand personality sections. For example, the people at the Corporation for Supportive Housing listed *persistence* in both sections. Once they saw the redundancy, they kept the term in their core values and used another trait for their personality. If a trait is truly a core value of your company—as accountability is for Dell, for instance—it will show up in everything you do and won't need to be reiterated in your brand personality. Now, when describing your brand personality, you can use another word that might add another dimension to your brand that didn't exist before. So, create the one sheet of paper and make sure that the skeleton of your brand roadmap is solid before you start adding the meat. Once you've done this, we can start talking about laying out the information in a way that's easy to understand.

THE OVERALL LAYOUT

The format presented in figure 6-1 is the most basic form of the brand roadmap. It consists of eight 8-by-11-inch sheets of paper printed on both sides, three-hole punched, and then put into a three-hole binder with a clear front. The information is presented in discrete sections and follows a logical, linear format. This simple structure allows people to understand each section and the interrelatedness of each section. Some companies never modify this basic structure. They print out the roadmaps on a color laser printer, and

FIGURE 6 - 1

Brand Roadmap Layout

This template is the simplest way to lay out the information in your brand roadmap. Start with this generic layout, and later in the process, you can customize the design of your brand roadmap to fit your particular brand.

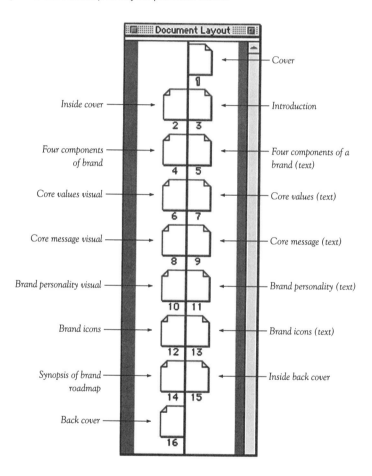

they're perfectly happy with this simple format. Other companies take the basic roadmap to their design firm and then have it re-designed and printed like a brochure. Both approaches work. Right now, however, we just want to make sure that your thinking and point of view are presented as clearly as possible so that there's as little room for misinterpretation as possible. The format is divided into the following eight parts:

1. The cover
2. The inside cover and introduction
3. The four components of a brand explained
4. Your core values
5. Your core message
6. Your brand personality
7. Your brand icons
8. Synopsis

Your roadmap may also include these optional components:

• Brand opportunities

• FAQ section

• Brand commandments

You'll notice that there are no more than two pages allowed for each section. That's not by accident. It forces companies to get to the point and state the information simply. For visual consistency, put a visual on the left-hand page and the text on the right. That's the template we'll be using throughout this chapter. Ultimately, we don't want this booklet to be any longer than it has to be to communicate effectively. Disciplining yourself at this stage will make sure that your roadmap will stay clear and to the point.

The Cover

The cover of your brand roadmap is the first chance you have to start communicating with the person who needs to read it. It should entice people to read further. Simplifying your brand message down to a single visual helps. CarClub.com printed its name out of a collage of hundreds of faces of ordinary people to communicate the "club" feeling of its brand. Jerome's Bar-B-Que used a fingerprint made of barbecue sauce and Jerome's slogan "The heart and soulfood of Petaluma" (figure 6-2). A Home Away From Homelessness simply used its logo—a colorful piece of artwork created by a homeless child—to communicate the fun, creative, positive qualities of their organization. Use whatever you feel captures the essence of your brand. Think of the cover as a poster. When it's done correctly, the cover will invite people to read the rest of the brand roadmap, which won't feel like the typical text-heavy strategy document.

FIGURE 6 - 2

Jerome's Bar-B-Que

This is the inside cover and introduction page of Jerome's Bar-B-Que brand roadmap. These elements set the tone for the whole document. The folder and fingerprint are barbecue-colored and the text was printed on natural parchment paper. The slogan "The heart and soulfood of Petaluma" and the dripping of barbecue sauce gave the roadmap an authentic feel. This kind of introduction makes people want to read on.

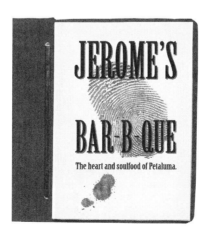

The Inside Cover and Introduction

You can utilize the inside cover and introduction page in different ways, depending on what you need to accomplish with your specific brand. Sometimes articulating the problem or opportunity that exists for your company is especially helpful for the people within your company who don't really understand what branding is or how it applies to them. Schools, nonprofit groups, and small businesses tend to fall into this camp and think of branding as too commercial, corporate, or expensive for their organization. In these instances, having a page that clearly defines why your organization needs branding is very helpful. A perception-versus-reality chart can be an effective element to demonstrate what perceptions an organization is looking to change with its brand roadmap. A quote from the company CEO defining how branding is going to help accomplish the mission of the company is also effective. It makes people feel as if the brand roadmap is coming from the top of the company and not just the marketing or research department.

For companies that already understand branding, a good quote to use is "The quality of a brand is determined by the promises made and the promises kept."[1] The quote sits on the introduction page with a visual of the company's logo, or maybe the key products on the inside cover. The words remind people that in order for any company to be a quality brand, the information the brand roadmap articulates needs to be executed throughout all departments and in all circumstances.

Crystallizing the importance and necessity of the brand roadmap for your company is the goal of the two introductory pages. Time spent on these pages is therefore well spent.

The Four Components of a Brand Explained

After the introduction, it's important to tell people the four areas you'll be covering and the importance of making sure that those areas work together. A good way to do this is to use the following definitions and place them on the right-hand page of the roadmap.

> *A brand is made up of four components:*
>
> Core values: *The values our brand is built on. Core values are the foundation of our company and the pillars of every message we deliver.*
>
> Brand message: *The overall key message we're trying to communicate. All other messages should support and add credibility to this message.*
>
> Brand personality: *The overall tone and attitude we use to deliver our message. Brand personality is the key emotional component that determines whether we're a likable brand.*
>
> Brand icons: *The executional tools we use to deliver our brand message and brand personality: for example, colors, typefaces, voice-over, logo, layouts, and music. Brand icons are the elements that make all our marketing materials uniquely us.*
>
> *When these elements are delivered in a consistent and cohesive manner, we have the building blocks of a long-term, successful brand.*

On the left-hand page, across the page from the preceding descriptions, we have often used the visual of four interlocked puzzle pieces because it's an easily understood representation of the interlocking nature of the core values, core message, brand personality, and brand icons (figure 6-3). If your company has certain corporate

FIGURE 6 - 3

United You Brand

There are numerous ways to show the interrelationship between the core values, core message, brand personality, and brand icons, but this visual works really well. The puzzle used for A Home Away From Homelessness was red, green, blue, and orange-yellow. Various shades of a single color are also appropriate when a company has one dominant color. This visual emphasizes that the four brand pieces need to work together.

colors, you can use those colors in the puzzle. If your company has one specific color, use shades of that color. Using the company's colors starts to make the brand roadmap feel less generic and more specific to that particular company.

If the puzzle piece visual doesn't work for you, there are lots of other ways to go. For example, the Corporation for Supportive Housing used a blueprint of the four cornerstones of a building since the organization was involved with helping create housing for the chronically homeless. However you decide to do it, the visual should communicate that the four components need to work together if the brand is going to succeed.

At this stage, it's better to be clear than obtusely creative. You can always hire a designer or an illustrator to come up with other ways to portray the four components, but for the purposes of this exercise, use the puzzle visual as a simple, tested visual.

Your Core Values

Once you've completed the overall brand components pages, it's time to explain how each component is unique to your company. The core values section will be the first section in your brand roadmap. Covering your company's core values gives people an overall context for the information that follows. It also focuses people on what's important about your specific brand. That way, when they don't see the exact traits or wording they might have liked in the other sections of the brand roadmap, they will still have an overall picture of your brand that gives them a context for the decisions you've made. When they understand the forest for the trees, many times they'll forgo their own personal preferences and buy into the overall direction of the brand.

Start by listing the three or four values you've decided upon, and organize those values on the right-hand side of the page. Then follow each value with a short description. If the text starts going longer than one page, you should edit it to get the information on one page rather than extending the text onto the visual page. Since the discipline of simplifying the information has worked for the brand roadmap of a multidimensional, multilayered, international brand like Dell Computer, it will certainly work for most of the companies reading this book. Be ruthless in your editing. Take the time to capture the true essence of what you're trying to say.

Once you have your core values listed, think about a visual or several visuals that might reinforce those core values. If you can, find a visual that makes people nod their heads and say, "Yes, I believe our company represents those values." It could be a visual of a newspaper or magazine article that highlights the organization's vision. It could be a visual of a survey or an award that proves the quality of your company's products or service. Pictures of people within your organization who epitomize your core values are another way to communicate what's important to your company. They remind people which core values are rewarded, both financially and with public recognition. The pictures also put a human face on your company and add a bit of humanity to your brand roadmap.

Sometimes pictures and quotes from the past can be very powerful reminders of a company's core values. For example, a visual of Thomas Edison combined with one of his quotes could be a powerful way to communicate General Electric's core value of innovation. Such a visual would definitely cement the notion that innovation was, is, and always will be a cornerstone of the GE brand. Using your company's history is a powerful reminder of the importance of sticking with something over time to create meaningful differentiation in the marketplace. In some cases, the values you're articulating can only be proven over time. Nordstrom's didn't become known for exceptional service overnight (in that case, a picture of an original Nordstrom's service ad from the early 1900s might be a good visual). Nor did Volvo become synonymous with safety overnight. Core values that have their roots in the company's past have a credibility that's hard to duplicate with new companies.

What core values are timeless for your company? Are there any visuals that remind people of those values? You can always put a caption with the visual to explain why that particular picture is indicative of your company's core values. Once you're comfortable that you've captured your core values both visually and verbally, you'll follow that with your core message.

Your Core Message

Take your core message, and put it on the right-hand page. Then write two or three paragraphs stating why you've chosen this message as your core brand message. In those paragraphs, you'll need to create a compelling argument to get people to understand this message. Since it's the one message that all other messages will refer back to, you'll want to make sure that people understand it and buy into it. Some companies talk about how their core message will differentiate them in the marketplace. Other companies reiterate how a particular message has worked for x number of years for their company. If you're having a hard time narrowing down your argument, pretend that you're sitting across the table from the most skeptical person in your organization. Now try to create a simple, thirty-second rationale for your message. Or imagine having the core-message conversation with one of your customers or investors. Doing that exercise should help you focus your thoughts on the most informative, compelling aspects of your message.

Next, choose the visual or visuals you want to use to demonstrate the core message, and put them on the left-hand side of the roadmap. I've mentioned historical images, but you can use contemporary visuals as well. You might use a current television commercial, for instance, that really captures the message of your company. Because television is such a high-profile medium, a commercial that really stands out in the culture can be a great way to remind people what message the world is getting about your company. The Kia brand roadmap, for instance, was filled with quite a few visuals from its television commercials. The use of these TV visuals made the brand roadmap feel like an integral part of the Kia brand. When the core message is clearly represented in the marketing materials—television commercials, Web sites, logos, print ads, products, annual reports—it can showcase the power of integrating the core message with the brand personality and brand icons. Which are, coincidentally, the next two sections in your brand roadmap.

Your Brand Personality

Write down the four or five personality traits that you completed at the end of chapter 3, and put them on the right-hand page. Be sure to include the descriptions. Then, place your visual or visuals on the left-hand side.

Using visuals of people can demonstrate that your brand personality is more like a person than a company. If you have a high-profile CEO or an owner who represents your brand personality, use a picture of him or her. Real-life photos capture the person's true personality rather than the typical annual-report-type staged shots. If your brand personality is represented by your customers (e.g., Oakland Raiders fans), a cartoon character (the Michelin Man), or a cultural icon (the Marlboro cowboy), use these real or imaginary people to bring your brand personality to life.

If you don't use a person, then make sure whatever visuals you do use truly capture the essence of your brand personality. If you're a brand that loves animals (e.g., Purina, Meow Mix), then use pictures of animals. Provocative brands, such as Benneton and Amnesty International, might employ a visual that challenges the reader. If you're a brand that's rugged (think Timberland, Craftsman tools), your visuals should embody that ruggedness. Visuals can really bring your brand personality to life. They will give people a visceral sense of the tone and attitude you want represented throughout your brand. You can start by looking through all your marketing materials to see which visuals capture your brand personality particularly well. You can usually find at least one or two items that have a distinctive spark to them. If there aren't any, find some that do have a spark (stock photography houses are a good place to start) and that capture the feeling you're trying to communicate.

Your Brand Icons

Once you have completed the two-page personality section of your roadmap and included some visuals, you're ready to create the brand icon section. Putting the text on the right-hand page and the visuals on the left-hand side has worked up to this point, but you now might wish to add a little variation. If you have more than five or six brand icons, you might put a description next to each icon to tie the two more closely together. For example, you could inset your logo into the paragraph that describes the relevance of your logo to your brand. Or if you want to leverage a specific architectural feature, you might want to show a small visual that goes with that description. It all depends on how literal you want to be about lining up each icon with each description. Sometimes, when you have a lot of brand icons, the pages can look confusing and crowded if you try to put all the text on the right and all the visuals on the left. It's more important to be clear than to be consistent with the previous sections of the brand roadmap.

If you've followed the steps in chapter 5, some of your icons are already clearly evident in the brand roadmap. For example, the brand roadmap should incorporate the same typefaces that you're asking people to use everywhere else. Your brand colors can also be used throughout the roadmap. The brand roadmap for Jerome's Bar-B-Que used barbecue colors. Home Away's roadmap used its colors to highlight the headings and subheads. A distinctive photographic style can also be used in your roadmap if it's a brand icon and it's used in all your other marketing materials. Simple, colorful, posterlike illustrations were used for the Dell roadmap because that was the corporate look at the time.

In the case of major or minor icons that might not be innately visual—smell, sound, or feel, for instance—adding visuals that highlight that particular sense can be used. For example, to highlight the importance of smell for the Starbucks brand, a closely-cropped visual of freshly ground coffee beans could work. In the case of showcasing the texture of a brand like Velcro, photographing the actual texture would reinforce the uniqueness of its brand icon. Sound is particularly difficult to illustrate visually, but showing a frame from a particular television commercial that uses a distinctive mnemonic or your theme music could work (e.g., United Airlines). Every icon doesn't need a visual, but sometimes it helps people get a better sense of which icons are important to the brand. If a visual doesn't clarify a particular icon, or if it makes the page cluttered or confusing, it's best to forgo a visual and just put down the explanation in text only. The important thing is to use this opportunity to turn your roadmap into a visual smorgasbord of your brand icons. If you have a hard time creating that feeling with the visuals you have at your disposal, pass along the information to your design firm or ad agency, either of which can help make sure your brand roadmap looks like your brand. Using brand icons throughout the brand roadmap will also signal that all your company's documents—even strategy documents like the brand roadmap—can be mirrors of your brand.

If you're having a hard time keeping the brand icons to two pages, then go to four. A common technique is to highlight the major icons on the first two pages and the minor icons on the next two. There are no hard and fast rules, but make sure you aren't going to four pages just because you don't want to take the time to edit your thoughts. Keep Mark Twain's quote in the back of your mind: "If I had more time, I would have written you a shorter letter."

Synopsis

The synopsis is a one-page encapsulation of the brand roadmap. It's a bulleted list of the key values, message, personality traits, and icons. It's a bare bones distillation of the brand roadmap that still communicates the essence of the brand. Use the synopsis as the shorthand version of the brand roadmap that you can pass along to someone when you don't want to give the person the whole document. It can also be a daily reminder on people's bulletin boards to remind them of the key points your brand is built upon. Think of it as a brand cheat sheet.

With the synopsis finished, you now have the basic model of the brand roadmap. The simplest version, a sixteen-page version, usually provides enough information to be an effective roadmap. You can then decide if you want to include any other sections in your brand roadmap. Sometimes, companies like to add a section that addresses specific brand opportunities, an FAQ section, or a list of brand commandments. We'll briefly look at the advantages of adding these sections to your brand roadmap.

Brand Opportunities

In the process of creating your brand roadmap, you might have seen some new opportunities that made sense for your brand. They could be ideas that help your company create new products, new services, clearer communications, or different sensory stimuli that could make the customer's brand experience a more meaningful one. Presenting ideas for new opportunities in your roadmap is an effective way to start people thinking along the lines you want them to think. It also gives them something specific to relate to. Whenever I've added this section to the brand roadmap, one or two ideas inevitably strike a chord in people and those ideas usually become a reality. For example, because of the company's renewed focus on steaks, Stuart Anderson's Black Angus created a whole new category of items on its menu, called "Reward Steaks." This new idea reinforced the company's passion for rewarding its customers with a great steak experience and also created a category of meals with higher profit margins. The Branson School used its brand opportunity section to show individual postcards highlighting the unique talents of the individual students and faculty who represented the diversity of the school. The idea of using individual postcards to create an ongoing relationship throughout the year with the organization's key audiences was also included in the brand opportunity sections of the Acoustic Disc and A Home Away From Homelessness road maps. Adding the specific examples and recommendations at the end of their brand roadmaps helped these companies create new materials that reinforced their brand roadmap as a useful, actionable tool for their company.

You'll find that by studying your competitors' Web sites, reading their marketing materials, and learning about their unusual services, you can sometimes generate ideas for your brand. Go ahead and include these ideas in your brand opportunity section; you can decide later whether they're doable. You can worry about budgets, feasibility studies, and how a particular idea fits into the next quarter's marketing plans later. For now, give your ideas a chance to live by putting them in this brand opportunity section.

Frequently Asked Questions

Including an FAQ section at the end of your brand roadmap can help prepare you for any possible questions or objections regarding the roadmap. It also lets people know that you took their real-world concerns into consideration when creating the document.

The most believable questions are those phrased exactly like how an employee might phrase them. For example, one question in a company's brand roadmap was "How does our brand message relate to the coupon ads we run in the Sunday paper every week?" The company used that question to talk about the need to balance short-term, tactical messages with an overall, long-term branding message. The company emphasized how the brand personality and specific brand icons could be used within the coupons to help reinforce the brand perception of quality products without sacrificing short-term sales. Generally, the more honest and relevant the questions in the FAQ section, the more believable the roadmap. One good way to start an FAQ section is to list four or five questions that you believe will be asked and then to answer them as succinctly and directly as you can. If you have a hard time coming up with the questions by yourself, let someone else read the roadmap, and ask the person what questions he or she might have. If asked, people will usually give you some very specific and practical issues that need to be addressed. Getting someone else's input is a great opportunity to address issues that you might have missed. It's better to address them now than after you've printed *x* amount of brand roadmaps and found out that your roadmap is heavy on theory and light on practicality. If your brand roadmap isn't addressing the day-to-day needs of the people who have the opportunity to represent your brand, then you've missed a key opportunity to solidify your brand. Including an FAQ section in your roadmap can ensure that you won't miss that opportunity.

Brand Commandments

A brand commandments section can be a very effective way to drive home the passion of your values. Including a list of commandments can also give you the flexibility to point out what your brand stands for, and what it won't stand for.

Here's a sampling of brand commandments found in a variety of different roadmaps.

1. *Thou shalt not overpromise.* Our mantra is underpromise and overdeliver. Underpromise and overdeliver. Actions always speak louder than words. So when you get a hankering to use hype, get help. Or just stop, breathe, and repeat after me: Underpromise and overdeliver . . .

2. *Thou shalt not brag about insignificant competitive differences.* Bragging will make us seem petty. Address major issues, like lower prices, better service, and longer-lasting products. Those are things that consumers are looking for. And never run a comparative ad for revenge or to validate some corporate

sense of superiority. Consumers will see right through the motive.

3. *Thou shalt not get too elitist, artsy, or obtuse.* Our audience is a mainstream audience. Snobbery is the surest way to convince our audience that we're not talking to them. Therefore, we must keep an unpretentious attitude in the language we use, the artwork we commission, the directors we pick, the speakers we get at dealer meetings, and the talent we hire.

4. *Thou shalt not lie.* Even if you don't always tell the whole truth, never lie. Brands are built on trust. One lie can destroy that trust. We can't afford to destroy the trust we've built.

5. *Thou shalt not follow directly in the path of our competitors.* Our strength lies in doing things differently from how other companies are doing them. Zig while they zag. Zag while they zig. The first one into a customer's mind has the element of surprise. The second one is ripe for an ambush. Ye who refuse to follow this simple commandment shall end up in the valley of marketing darkness, never to be seen again.

6. *Thou shalt not shun fun.* This is a serious business, with serious money at stake, and serious marketing decisions to be made—for us. For the customers, it's a time for them to feel good about themselves, to feel good about their purchase, and to feel good about our brand. So let them. Always deliver our serious messages in a fun way. Seriously.

7. *Thou shalt not be inscrutable.* We need to communicate openly with ourselves, the press, our customers, and our various partners. Silence breeds paranoia. Silence breeds thoughts that are not conducive to building the open, honest brand we want to build. Being inscrutable is intolerable.

8. *Thou shalt not be a fence straddler.* We have no room or patience in our company for people who refuse to act until all the facts are in, because they're the people who inevitably refuse to act at all. All the facts will never be in. We want people with the intelligence and confidence to gather the available information, have a point of view, defend that point of view, and then act upon their conviction. If you're a fence straddler, your job is in the balance.

9. *Thou shalt not kill ideas indiscriminately.* New ideas fuel our innovation. They're precious commodities that need a little nurturing. Just because an idea doesn't come out fully born like some Mozart concerto doesn't mean it's not a good idea. Whether you come up with an idea or someone else does, honor the idea, sleep on it, and improve it. We need all the ideas we can get. As Alain (Emile Auguste Chartier) said, "Nothing is more dangerous than an idea when it's the only one you've got."

10. *Thou shalt not get bogged down with too many shalt-nots.* Despite these commandments, it's important that we remain open to changing the rules. Not haphazardly, indiscriminately, or individually, but together. In the constantly changing world of marketing, we must remain open to new possibilities when others start to confuse our consumer by coveting what we have created.

Feel free to use any or all of the preceding commandments. Better yet, have some fun and create commandments of your own. Try to keep each commandment more general than specific. In other words, don't chastise a person for not answering the phone on the first ring if that's the one thing that bugs you. Rephrase it into something like "Thou shalt not be unresponsive." Then you can use the phone example if you want to illustrate your point. By reinforcing the core value of responsiveness, you've opened the door for people to apply that concept to whatever they're doing, not just answering the phone. If you can also deliver the commandments with a little attitude and a sense of humor, you can add some personality and humanity to the overall roadmap.

THE ULTIMATE TEST

Now comes the million-dollar question for anyone creating a brand roadmap: How would you feel if a competitor owned the ideas in your brand roadmap? This question can keep a marketing director up at night, but if the question doesn't make you sweat, then you probably haven't asked tough enough questions when creating your brand roadmap.

The converse of that question is "How would your competitors feel if they knew you could own your brand roadmap ideas in the marketplace?" Putting yourself in your competitors' shoes is a good way to look objectively at your brand roadmap. If you can imagine them lying awake at night with that thought, then you've got a powerful brand roadmap.

Either question should give you a more objective viewpoint on the impact and viability of your brand roadmap. After all, if done correctly, your brand roadmap will be the template for winning both the hearts and the minds of customers, prospects, and employees for years to come. That alone is worth asking the tough questions now.

CONCLUSION

Before you leave this book, take this opportunity to evaluate your brand roadmap from an overall, executional point of view. For example, if you're a visual brand, like Polaroid or Nikon, you might want to make sure your roadmap is heavily visual. If your brand is trying to change its image from a product-oriented brand to a people-oriented brand, see if that "peopleness" is coming through in your roadmap. If you're a sophisticated brand, then make sure that the whole feel of your brand roadmap is sophisticated. Using artistic, black-and-white photography, Beringer Winery designed its brand roadmap to look like an oversized coffee-table book. These kinds of touches can give people an overall feeling for the brand that can't always be expressed in words. The brand roadmap then becomes that much closer to being a true mirror of your brand.

Chances are, if you have conscientiously followed the roadmap-making process outline in this book, you will have created a roadmap as valuable as the ones created by the companies with whom I've worked. You should have a living, breathing branding document that can be used throughout your organization. Live with it for a few weeks before you commit it to a final printing. Get input from all the people who will be affected by the conclusions in your brand roadmap. Tweak whatever issues consistently come up for people. This isn't about who's right or wrong; it's about creating a document that everyone feels works for the brand. The more that people feel the roadmap represents the whole company and not just one person, the more they will take ownership of the ideas in the roadmap.

It's time to congratulate yourself. Creating a workable brand roadmap is not an easy job. To do it well, you need to spend a good amount of time and focused attention, commodities that are becoming rarer and rarer in today's business world. So sit back and enjoy your accomplishment: You've taken a giant step toward making your brand more grounded, more relevant, and more cohesive. Capturing the essence of your brand and putting it into a form that's clear and concise will help ensure that your brand has the tools necessary to be seen, heard, and remembered in the marketplace for years to come.

NOTES

PREFACE

1. Nicholas Ind, *Living the Brand* (Dover, NH: Kogan Page, 2001), 75.
2. David A. Aaker, *Building Strong Brands* (New York: Free Press, 1996).
3. Every ad we prepared for Dell had a separate 800 number so that we could track specific orders, magazine effectiveness, ad placement effectiveness, target markets, and specific offers. At the time I left the business, our ad agency was doing over four hundred ads a year for Dell.

CHAPTER 1

1. Ind, *Living the Brand*, 15.
2. "Nike Announces Anti-Sweatshop Initiative," This Week's Sweatshop News, 14 May 1998, <http://www.uniteunion.org/sweatshops/ newsthisweek/5-14-98.html> (accessed 9 September 2002).
3. Theodore Levitt originally coined the term *marketing myopia*. Mentioned in Harry Beckwith's *Selling the Invisible* (New York: Warner Books, 1997), 36.

CHAPTER 2

1. Gary Gusick and I initially wrote the line for an Apple III advertisement. Unfortunately, it was a bit of an overpromise for the Apple III, to say the least. Consequently, the print ad was killed. Fortunately, our line was resurrected for the Macintosh television commercial. "1984"

then became a believable rallying cry because Apple had a message and a product that lived up to its core values.

2. James C. Collins and Jerry I. Porras, *Built to Last* (New York: Harper-Business, 1997), 223.

3. Bruce Horovitz, "Volvo, Agency Fined $150,000 Each for TV Ad Commercials," *Los Angeles Times,* 22 August 1991.

4. *America's Greatest Brands* (New York: America's Greatest Brands, 2001).

5. Bob Levenson, *Bill Bernbach's Book* (New York: Villard Books, 1987), 144.

6. Aaker, *Building Strong Brands,* 138. As an aside, in 1988 when my partner and I were judging "The Show," the annual Minneapolis advertising show, we awarded the Harley-Davidson tattoo ad a gold medal. The visual was a close-up of a Harley tattoo on a beefy man's arm, and the headline read, "When was the last time you felt this strongly about anything?" I love truth in advertising.

7. U.S. Navy, "The Core Values of the United States Navy," <http://www.chinfo.navy.mil/navpalib/traditions/html/corvalu.html> (accessed 27 February 2002).

8. *America's Greatest Brands,* 141.

9. Ibid., 73.

10. Corporation for Supportive Housing, Brand Roadmap, prepared by Mike Moser (29 April 2002).

11. A Home Away From Homelessness, Brand Roadmap, prepared by Mike Moser (7 January 2001).

CHAPTER 3

1. Al Ries and Jack Trout, *Positioning: A Battle for Your Mind* (New York: Warner Books, 1981), 8.

2. Howard Luck Gossage, *Is There Any Hope for Advertising?* (Chicago: University of Illinois Press, 1986), 4.

3. Steven Pinker, *How the Mind Works* (New York: W.W. Norton & Company, 1997), 90.

4. James L. Adams, *Conceptual Blockbusting,* 3 ed. (Boston: Addison-Wesley, 1986), 15.

5. Jon Steel, *Truth, Lies and Advertising* (New York: John Wiley & Sons, 1998).

6. Nicholas Samstag, *How Business Is Bamboozled by the Ad-Boys* (New York: James H. Heineman, 1966).

CHAPTER 4

1. Aaker, *Building Strong Brands,* 174.
2. David Ogilvy, *Confessions of an Advertising Man* (New York: Atheneum, 1980), 102.
3. Aaker, *Building Strong Brands,* 141.
4. Kia Motors America, Brand Roadmap, prepared by Goldberg Moser O'Neill (24 March 1998). The skeptics box was an inset on each page of the Kia brochure. The box voiced the customers' concerns about the Kia brand in their own words. The headings started with phrases like "C'mon. Why does America need another car?" "If someone slams into me, do I have a prayer?" We would then answer the questions about affordability, safety, and other attributes in a direct, honest way.
5. Dell Computer, Brand Roadmap, prepared by Goldberg Moser O'Neill (28 October 1998).
6. Stuart Anderson's, Brand Trailmap, prepared by Goldberg Moser O'Neill (22 March 1999).
7. Levenson, *Bill Bernbach's Book,* 100.
8. Beringer Winery, Brand Roadmap, prepared by Goldberg Moser O'Neill (2 April 1998).
9. A Home Away From Homelessness, Brand Roadmap, prepared by Mike Moser (7 January 2001).
10. ShareWave Brand Roadmap, prepared by Goldberg Moser O'Neill (22 October 1998).

CHAPTER 5

1. Ries and Trout, *Positioning,* 86.
2. Marc Gobe, *Emotional Branding* (New York: Allworth Press, 2001), 69.
3. Diane Ackerman, *A Natural History of the Senses* (New York: Vintage Books, 1991), 254–255.
4. Kit Hinrichs, *Typewise* (Cincinnati: North Light Books, 1990).
5. Ibid., 18.
6. Gobe, *Emotional Branding,* 73.
7. Ibid.

8. Ackerman, *A Natural History of the Senses*, 5.
9. Stuart Anderson's, Brand Trailmap, prepared by Goldberg Moser O'Neill (22 March 1999).
10. Dell Computer, Brand Roadmap, prepared by Goldberg Moser O'Neill (28 October 1998).
11. Acoustic Disc, Brand Roadmap, prepared by Mike Moser (16 January 2000).

CHAPTER 6

1. The original version of this quote came from my friend Tony Broadbent, who said, "A brand is determined by all promises made, all promises kept." I believe that his comment is true of the best brands, but I tweaked it a bit to incorporate brands that don't always do what they say they're going to do. They're brands, too, but just not the highest-quality brands.

INDEX

ABOUT THE AUTHOR

MIKE MOSER spent over twenty years in advertising as an art director, creative director, and finally a partner in his own agency, working on brands such as Apple, Dell, Cisco, Kia Motors, Dreyer's Ice Cream, Reebok, and California Cooler, to name just a few. He has won over 300 national and international advertising awards and was twice voted San Francisco Art Director of the Year. After leaving advertising—and his agency Goldberg Moser O'Neill—in 1999, he donated his time and talents to schools, nonprofits, and very small businesses that were having a hard time being seen and heard in this marketing-saturated culture. *United We Brand* is his first book, and an encapsulation of that experience.

Mike Moser is also a fine artist working in mixed media, collage, and assemblage. His first one-man show, Peace By Piece, was created at the same time as this book. The same process of collecting bits and pieces to create a unified image mirrored the goal of this book, which is teaching organizations how to collect their own bits and pieces and create a unified image in the marketplace.

He has three very smart, creative, talented kids—Mallory, Jack, and Henry—and a great relationship with his ex-wife—Frances—all of whom provide inspiration and feedback that allows his own fragmented pieces to find stability and "unitedness."